Fearless Ghosts

by

Alex Scott

BELLCODE BOOKS
10 Ridge Bank
Todmorden
West Yorkshire OL14 7BA

WARNING

This book makes references to the way Alex Scott and his friends crossed railway lines and entered railway depots without permission, at times putting themselves in great danger.

Trespassing on railway property was a dangerous thing to do then and is even more dangerous nowadays as trains approach more quickly and silently than in the days of steam.

It is illegal and trespassers are prosecuted. Anyone who is hit by a train will almost certainly be killed or seriously disabled for the rest of their life.

In no way does Bellcode Books, by publishing this material, condone trespass, in fact quite the reverse. In some of the stories Alex is injured by his own foolhardy actions and the story of Little Kevin shows just how life-threatening messing about on railway property can be.

Published 1999 by Bellcode Books, 10 Ridge Bank, Todmorden, West Yorkshire OL14 7BA

ISBN 1 871233 12 7

Printed in England by The Amadeus Press Ltd., 517 Leeds Road, Huddersfield, West Yorkshire HD2 1YJ.

MASTERS AND BOYS - BIRCHFIELD ROAD SECONDARY MODERN, MIDWAY 1960 - 1964.
Headmaster: J. Holdham; deputy head: Mr. Tallyntyne; Mr. Davies, geography; Mr. Dixon, maths; Mr. Evans, English; Mr. Jenkins, science; Mr. Jones, sports and maths; Mr. Lane, metalwork; Mr. Davis, technical drawing; Mr. Lowe, music; Mr. Obungwanna; Mr. Taylor, R.E. and music; Mr. Thompson, art; Mr. Phillips and Mr. Williams: woodwork and light engineering. To those forgotten, I'm truly sorry.

CLASSMATES between the above dates remembered, some unfortunately forgotten - sorry - Barry Sayers, Bobby Johnson, Colin Sutton, Colin Trueman, David Hanna, David Weston, Daley Kanutte, David Burrows, Frankie Avantargearto, Jimmy Phillips, John 'Ossie' Osborne, Johnny Raybone, Leslie Smyth, Melvin Davies,Mervin Powell, Paul Cowalski, Paul Pipper, Peter Pipper, Peter Mertins. Also Larry, Benjamin, Layley, Chapman, Morris and about 20 other lads I can't recall.

Contents

Arriving in Aston   Page 4

The 'jack-in-the-box' class   Page 10

The field of pleasure   Page 15

Tasting 'the smoke'   Page 21

Melvin's masterpiece   Page 26

A risky ride   Page 29

The railway enthusiast   Page 37

The works party   Page 40

Holiday money   Page 46

Vandals!   Page 52

Injury & insults   Page 56

Cut short   Page 59

Trouble in school   Page 61

Waggers   Page 67

The visitor   Page 71

The Newport incident   Page 81

The cold wind of change   Page 93

Troubled times in Wigan   Page 99

The man from the BBC   Page 104

Little Kevin   Page 109

The treble chance   Page 113

A working man   Page 116

Pushing our luck   Page 127

The best yet   Page 131

A brush with the law   Page 136

A bad move   Page 144

With special thanks to Melvin, David, Spinner, Nicky, Eamon, Gerry and all my friends for their companionship, to all the shed foremen, the guards and railwaymen for putting up with us so cheerfully, and especially to my wife Carol for her support during my endless hours at the word processor.

ARRIVING IN ASTON

Another rumble of thunder rolled down the Lichfield Road. There was nothing unusual about this, it always seemed to be thundering down there. I asked my dad about it and he just laughed and told me it wasn't the same as the thunder we got during thunder storms.

"The thunder you can hear is coming from the trains that pass over the railway bridge down at Aston station," he said, still chuckling at my innocence.

Time passed until one day I felt the pulling of my body down towards Aston station, a force, a presence? I don't know - it just happened.

I found myself walking down the Lichfield Road. Once I reached the open doors of Aston station this pulling of my person took me very slowly up the wooden stairs to the old boarded platform. There was nothing to see, nothing to do. No trains in the station, no trains coming or going - what was I doing here?

Then, suddenly, the answer. A whistle made me jump. The sudden noise scared me. Looking to my left, I could see this small, dark looking train coming towards me. It stopped on the opposite platform. A brick wall stopped me backing away any further - this little train didn't look so little now. I felt it was looking me over.Then it gave a shrill whistle and huffed and puffed away. My neck stretched out as my eyes followed it out of sight. I felt a lot happier once it had gone but now, in the distance to my far right, I could see more trains. All this stretching nearly made me fall onto the track.

The force was now pulling my scrawny little body back down the stairs, over the main road, and under the railway bridge, my legs whizzing me up Holborn Hill. I came to a grinding halt because I was now confronted by a very high wall next to an dirty old derelict factory. The windows had seen better days, well those that weren't smashed, anyway.

I was trying unsuccessfully to climb this high wall when two passers-by noticed my feeble efforts.

"Want a lift up, sonny?," the man asked.

"Oh, yes please," I answered.

"Wanna see the trains do ya?," he asked me.

"Cor, yeah. Yeah please mister."

They gave me a bunk up. I thanked them and just sat on the wall looking at the trains in front of me. Like the factory, they looked dark and dirty.

The little trains moved off in all directions. The bigger ones made a lot more noise; they seemed to be in no mood for being moved. Some of them had blinkers, like the milkman's horse.

I must have sat there for an hour when suddenly a voice from down below startled me.

"Oi. oi you up there. What ya doing on?"

I turned very carefully and saw this chap dressed in blue-ish overalls and wearing a cap looking up in my direction. He was waving his finger at me and telling me to get down. He helped me down and then set about telling me off and asking me what I was doing up there in the first place.

Once he had finished ticking me off, I, with quivering words, explained that I was only watching the trains. I was shaking a bit as he towered over me. He marched me off down the hill, telling me off all the way, his finger wagging continuously.

It was a long telling off. Then again, it was a long hill.

We reached the bottom of Holborn Hill. His final words to me were: "If I ever catch you here again my lad, you'll be for the high jump."

I thought to myself: "I couldn't climb that wall, everlone jump it."

"Now, off you get," he said.

I walked slowly up the Lichfield Road, glancing over my shoulder a couple of times. He watched me all the way, until he was out of sight.

The next few years passed me by until an accident forced my whole family to move from Aston.

One night we were woken up by a very bad thunder storm. Mom, Dad, my sister Sheila and myself were brought downstairs. We all sat in the front door area watching the heavy rain fall. Even in the early hours the heat from the storm made the atmosphere very warm indeed. Then there was a crash and parts of our chimney fell into the very small box-like garden. We never knew until later that morning that lightning had struck not only the chimney pot, but the roof just over my little box bedroom. There were large lumps of masonry on my mattress - killed a few bed bugs, I bet.

I slept on the sofa for the rest of that night. In the morning, the damage to the whole area could be seen from over at my Uncle Fred's house. My dad went down the next alleyway to see the damage for himself from the other side. He came back and informed our mom that it looked bad and we must get in touch with the council. A chap from the housing department came along and he decided that the house had to be evacuated for at least six weeks. This was no problem for us as all our relatives lived down the grove. Fred just opposite us, Nan next-door, Charlie in the last house along from Fred.

Our spanking brand new roof and chimney were the talking point of our grove and people, having heard the extended version of what happened that night, came to see for themselves what the fuss was about.

Apparently, a young lad had been dragged by the skin of his teeth from the rubble, a fireman had saved his life and the police had cordoned off the street to get an ambulance to his rescue.

How could such a story get around, I wonder?

I was born on a Saturday night, 19th September, 1948, in this very small back-to-back - a posh description for a slum. In attendance were my mom(of course), Joan Agnus, Mary Scott, Nan Sinderberry - my mom's mom, Maud - my father's mom, and an excellent doctor - Dr. Gold. The midwife? Sorry, don't know.

An outside bar had been well stocked by the thirsty members of our family plus neighbours, friends, friends of friends and a very welcome bunch of excuse onlookers - the pubs had shut by this time.

Present were my dad, Billy - well not just yet - his brothers Charlie and Fred, Grandad Eddie - my mom's father - Aunt Leah, her husband Charlie and their daughters Patty and Jean. Rose Hartley would haunt me if she was not mentioned, plus her husband George - our lovable local rogue.

A fine selection of torches and candles lit up the small garden - well, you do have to see what you're drinking - also who you're drinking with, who came with whom and who left with whom.

At 11.45pm Alex was out and a big cheer rang out down our grove, not so much for me - just so the party could begin. We were visited by two boys in blue. Of course, they had to sample the goods - can't have any party goers poorly now, can we? They were great, those lads, nothing to worry about when those boys from the local cop shop at Victoria Road were around.

Everyone was still swigging until the early hours of Sunday morning. One or two bodies found the living room floor very early on. You didn't invite people, they just came. Doors were never closed, never locked - happy days.

On that Sunday afternoon the Queens pub was packed out with on-going party people. The booze flowed like a river and the lav overflowed like the river had burst its banks. Just think if my mom had given birth to twins - the party would still be going on.

I grew up like most of the kids down the grove, a dirty, scruffy, runny nosed, skinny little mite. There was more meat on a sparrow than me. If I lay flat in my bed my mom thought there was no-one in it.

The early years passed and my first day at school came round. I was taken to meet the head mistress at Sycamore Road infants, one Mrs. Moss. She had purple hair, like an early punk rocker. She welcomed me to her school and said I would like it there.

My mom gave me a kiss in front of four hundred other kids. I watched her leave the school hall, then I watched all the other kids standing about. Many had noisy instruments in their little mitts - triangles, penny whistles, tambourines, little toy drums and anything else that could make a sound.

The time was now 8.55 and the thinking behind these instruments was soon to become clear. Mrs. Moss made her way onto the stage, wished all and sundry a good morning. Everyone shouted at the top of their little voices: "Good morning Mrs. Moss."

She then placed a black whistle to her lips, gave out a blast and what followed frightened me so much that at approximately 9.01, young Alex was back in his house with his mom, crying.

The idea was simple, Mrs. Moss's whistle was the signal for the whole school to make as much noise as humanly possible, to make sure everybody in the school hall was awake. I froze for a minute, then headed for the nearest exit, out of the school, over the road and home.

I blurted out, between sniffing and snorting and using my sleeve as a handkerchief, just what had happened and why I was back home so soon. My mom thought it all very funny and by 9.15 poor Alex was back at the loony farm.

Mrs. Moss thought it strange for me to run away home. My mom kissed me 'tarrar' for the second time while Mrs. Moss took my hand and led me off to meet my first ever teacher, one Mrs. Smith.

I remember from my first meeting with this horrible woman I was not a liked little lad. At times, you meet people in life and for some unknown reason you just don't like them and Mrs. Smith didn't like me.

She would not have me in her lesson and each morning after register she sent me outside to stand underneath the clock overlooking the school hall.

This went on for three months and I never knew anything about the lessons she taught. I learnt nothing, except how to tell the time.

One day, by chance, my mom came into school to see Mrs. Moss. Seeing me stood under the clock she called to me: "Alex, Alex. What are you standing there for?"

I just shrugged my shoulders.

"Don't know, bin standing here for about three months, well ever since I came to this school, Mom," I told her.

After having me, my mom was a rather large lady but when she was slim, I was told later in life, you never messed with her as she would, if need be, land you one. On hearing my reason, or rather the lack of it, for standing under the clock, she went absolutely crackers.

The classroom door nearly came off its hinges as it flew open, desks and the old school blackboard and easel crashed to the floor. Children ran out into the hall crying and screaming for fear of their little lives. Mrs. Smith was by now being strangled by my mom who gave this woman such a walloping before Mrs. Moss and the other teachers arrived. Her hair was a mess, her clothes were hanging off her shoulders, she had a cut mouth - my mom would have killed her that day but for the intervention of the other staff. As for me, I just stood there under the clock, listening and laughing.

The teachers finally dragged my mom off this poor woman and when, after some time, they had managed to calm the situation down, Mrs. Smith, plus escort, and my mom, plus escort, were taken to Mrs. Moss's private office.

Mrs. Moss asked Mrs. Smith why she did not allow me into her class during lesson time. Mom told us she never really offered an explanation and this left Mrs. Moss in a very awkward situation which gave her very little choice but to warn Mrs. Smith about her future conduct. My mom was also warned by Mrs. Moss about her conduct and the way in which she just went for Mrs. Smith. Mrs. Moss said Mom could have caused Mrs Smith some very serious injuries and a full report would have to be sent to the School Board. She then pointed out the severity of the School Board being notified.

The tale of the School Strangler soon spread around the grove and for years the neighbours played on it.

"Look out, Joan's on the loose, shut your doors. Blimey, grab the kids, it's the Strangler," they'd tease.

My mom just laughed it off but people would stop her in the grove, just to ask her to tell them about the day she nearly strangled Mrs. Smith.

Mrs. Smith was as nice as pie to me after that day. Nothing was mentioned to the School Board and nothing was ever heard of this incident ever again. Well, apart from Mom stretching the tale out when neighbours wanted a free giggle.

The next event came when my sister Sheila was born and that was our family complete

Twice a year, my Nan and Grandad took me to Blackpool and 1956 was no exception. They looked after me for most of my childhood. I never knew why and I never asked. I was too young to understand some things, too young to want to. Life for me was a child's life, just a snotty-nosed kid from Aston.

The train ride from Birmingham New Street to Blackpool was just a case of me sitting in a compartment with my Nan and Grandad, some sweets, pop and my comics to read on the way. It would be a few more years before I discovered what was really out there but when I did discover it, my adventures would take me far and wide.

Half way through 1960, the council told us that we were being moved out of Aston, to a brand new maisonnette in another part of Birmingham, Perry Bar.

Now, as we know, any excuse for a really good booze-up was never passed over and once word got round that we were leaving, everyone in the grove, regulars and outsiders, chipped in towards a grand variety of drinks, snap and trimmings, just like at Christmas.

The party over, we were on our way to Perry Bar. My mom took hours saying goodbye, more tears were spilt than drinks were drunk that day. I only ever saw them all again on the odd visit we made.

We took time settling into our new home. Many of our new neighbours were on speaking terms straight away and were soon exchanging reasons for leaving their old houses behind. We lived on the upper floor of the block and were quickly on talking terms with the first two families to move in on the same landing. They were Mr. and Mrs. Jones to our left, and Mr. and Mrs. Crawley to our right.

Eventually the block filled up and we all got to know each other. But there was one real difference from the old streets - everyone kept their doors closed and locked for most of the time, even when they were in. This was just one early change in people's habits that came with our new home. There were more to follow, for our community and for me.

Over the wall in Aston shed was a world of engines - big, small and some with blinkers like the milkman's horse. The ones with blinkers came no bigger than this - Class 9F 2-10-0 No. 92220 *Evening Star*, the last British Railways steam loco to be built, by the coal hopper on 24th June, 1962. *(Photo by Alex Scott)*

THE 'JACK - IN - THE BOX' CLASS

My first day at a new school - Birchfield Road Secondary Modern, and I found myself in a really strange class. They called it the "Jack-in-the-box" class. I didn't ask why, I thought time would reveal that secret.

The science class was up two floors and to the left it overlooked the railway lines that ran between Birmingham, Perry Bar and Walsall. When a train passed, the signal for certain pupils to jump up and down was given by a rather large boy. He would jump up, then sit straight back down and fiddle with a pen and a pad. Then the others would follow suit, hence the class nickname. The teacher would just look at these lads jumping up and down each time a train passed and shake his head from side to side. It's a wonder it never fell off.

I was later informed that the big lad's name was Melvin "Smelly" Davies. I don't know why he got the 'Smelly' bit, he never did smell. It was just one of those silly nicknames people got in school days.

Some time later, again in a science class and watching these lads jumping up and down watching the trains go by, my mind flashed back to that time in the 1950s when I saw the trains down at Aston station. Thinking about that chap telling me off made me smile in the middle of what was supposed to be a serious science lesson. More like a train watching lesson than science, this one.

A few days later, after being out shopping down Newtown Row, my mom and I were waiting for a bus back to Perry Bar, a 33, 51 or a 52, any of them would do. The bus stop was just opposite the Hipperdrome Theatre and close by was a shop selling rude magazines. The theatre showed girlie shows, hence the shop.

I was just glancing in the shop window when a book took my eye. My mom came up close behind me and gave me a clout round the earhole. Mom thought I was looking at the girlie mags. She called me a dirty little .....and threatened to tell my dad as soon as we got home. I protested and declared my innocence, so another clout came my way.

"I was looking at a train book, Mom," I sobbed.

She walked towards the shop, looked in the window, went inside and then came out again.

"That told him. Filth!," she snapped.

Next morning, I was up for school and Mom was making a fuss about the postman being late. She told me to look over the balcony and see if he was about. On the front door mat was a brown paper bag, folded very neatly.

"Only a brown paper bag Mom," I shouted.

"Look inside. What's in it?," she asked.

"No name on it Mom, nothing on it at all," I shouted again.

"Well have a look," she said. "Open it up and have a look."

I opened the bag up and a great big smile came across my face. A train book.

"Thanks Mom," I said and gave her a great big kiss. "Cor, thanks our Mom," I said again.

"That's for telling the truth," she said, "Sorry Alex."

The cover had an orange band, and a thicker green band with words written in black: "Ian Allan ABC British Railways Locomotives."

Below that was another orange band, then a small photograph of a Jubilee class steam locomotive.

Then came another orange band, another thin green band and the words written in black: "3, London Midland, Scottish Regions 2'6."

The first page inside the cover said "Winter 1960/61 edition"

I still have this book.

I couldn't wait to get to school. In fact, I went early just to catch Melvin Davies in the hope that he would tell me what to do with my new book.

The book was half in and half out of my pocket and I did not get very far into the school playground when the bigger kids grabbed it off me. They called me all sorts of names, some of which I had heard people being called and others I had never heard before.

Eventually, they gave me my book back. It was a bit bent. I suppose they thought I was as well with a train book.

I walked away still with them taunting me, calling me "train spotter, ... spotter."

My steps quickened and their taunts soon faded into the playground noise.

I was looking for Big Melvin. He would tell me how to go about this train spotting. I caught up with him and asked him, rather furtively, about the hobby. He looked around, took me into the school corridor, and explained as quick as the words could come from his mouth.

Then he hurried out through the doors, my thanks ringing in his ears.

"Great," I thought. "Must get a seat by the window."

As the lesson continued, Big Melvin would jump up, look out of the window and write the engine number down on his pad. Others in the group followed suit. I stood up last and was still looking for the engine number when Mr. Jenkins, our science teacher, called my name.

"Scott! What are you standing up for?"

My mom and dad always told me if ever you told a lie you would, if caught out, have to tell another to cover up the first one.

"I couldn't make out the engine number, sir, because the engine was so dirty. Sorry sir," I responded nervously.

"Mr. Davies, would you please stand up and tell another member of the train spotting group the engine number," Mr. Jenkins said.

"Yes sir," Melvin agreed to do this. He turned, gave me a dirty look and told me the number.

"Thankyou Davies. Now sit down," said Mr Jenkins. "Happy now, Scott?"

"Yes sir, sorry sir."

"That's that," I thought, "Melvin will give me a bashing outside. Any further information I may require as far as train spotting is concerned has gone."

I was the last person out of class. I hoped they had all gone home but Melvin and a few of his pals stood waiting for me.

"This is it," I thought. "A bashing from these classmates."

They walked towards me, looking straight at me. I felt my pulse begin to race.

"Any minute now will come the first wallop," I thought.

"We're off to town, first to New Street then to Snow Hill. Wanna come with us?" they asked, their expressions softening.

"I would like to, yeah, but I must ask my mom first. It's on the way. I only live two minutes walk from school."

"Right," they said, "let's go."

Mom was in and I told them to hang on for me.

She looked over the balcony at the boys waiting for me.

They looked back up and shouted: "Hello Mrs. Scott. Alex will be okay with us. We'll be back about seven."

She gave me a few pence for the bus and off we went.

I remember New Street from my holiday trips with Nan and Grandad but I had never been to Snow Hill before.

The entrance, with its circular pick-up and drop-off point, was something to see - I mean the fancy cars, some chauffeur-driven.

The station seemed to have an air of class about it, as did the people using it.

Melvin headed off in the direction of a small bright red machine attached to the outer wall near the platform entrance. He returned and gave us each a ticket.

"Follow me," he said. "We must get a move on."

We followed him past the ticket lady. He showed his ticket to her and we did the same. As soon as we were on the platform a train approached. We all jumped into a carriage, closed the door behind us and waited for the train to move off. It entered a very long tunnel and then emerged into the bright sunshine.

"Come on lads, look both sides," said Melvin.

The other two lads looked to the left, Melvin and I to the right. All the

12

time we were writing down the engine numbers we saw en-route to - but where were we going to?

"Look at all those engines, Melvin!," I exclaimed.

"Yes, it's Tyseley Loco," he replied.

The other two lads looked out of the carriage window on our side, scribbling down engine numbers as fast as was humanly possible.

"Ready lads!" Melvin shouted as soon as the train stopped. "Follow me, but stay close by. Alex, you stick with me and just do what I ask you to."

"Er, right Melv, will do."

We ran up the platform stairs, turned right at the top, then ran until we arrived in a large railway yard. There were coaches, wagons and engines all over the place.

"Alex, go and get those engines." Melvin gave me my instructions while pointing towards some engines near a very large coaling tower.

"After that, go and get the engines in the top yard then meet us over there." He pointed to a very large building.

I ran off writing down the numbers as fast as I could and then met up with Melvin at the place he told me.

"Come on," he said, "and look at this."

I found myself standing on a turntable with all the engines facing me. I was about to write them down when Melvin said: "Come on, there's two more like this."

"What about the numbers?," I asked

"Don't worry Alex, we've already got them. Come on, back to the station."

I took one last look before we headed off towards the station. What a sight - hundreds of engines all in one place.

Once we met up with the other lads we were off again on another train. We passed the shed with all the engines in and pulled into another station - Small Heath. We got off here, left the station and jumped on a number eight bus.

As the bus approached the bottom of a hill, Melvin commanded: "Right, same again!"

We got off and starting running again, following Melvin.

We arrived at another massive shed. This was 21A, Saltley. Again, Melvin told me where to go and where to meet up. I carried on and for the second time in a matter of minutes I was standing on a turntable. This was really fascinating. Again, Melvin looked in the direction of another two turntables.

"Come on, we must get a move on," he said.

We left the shed and ran up the hill. Just made it in time to jump on another train. We got off at, well, would you believe it, Aston station. We mingled in with the teatime passengers and then hurried across the busy main road up Holborn Hill.

I was a little taller this time but still we had to help each other over the high wall. Once more, Melvin pointed out the engines he wanted me to get.

Another shed done, we climbed back over the wall and ran back down the hill towards Aston station. By now my head was spinning.

We leaped back up the stairs just in time to catch another train. We arrived at Perry Bar station, waited for the crowd to move off, then very casually followed Melvin. A railwayman looked in our direction.

"We're just collecting train numbers," Melvin told him

"Right lads, okay," he said,

We moved well away from the station and Melvin and I started to exchange all the numbers we had seen. The other two lads shouted out different numbers. Melvin just said "okay, okay, okay."

This went on for some time, rather like the stock exchange, numbers every few seconds. Finally, Melvin gave me a very long list of numbers all written out very tidy on pieces of schoolbook paper. Then we parted company with the other lads.

"See you tomorrow in school lads," I said.

"Yes, okay Al see ya," they replied.

Melvin walked a little way with me and said he would bring something to school for me tomorrow. I thanked him for letting me come with him and the other two lads.

"Okay," he said. "See ya tomorrow."

It was well after seven when I arrived home. Mom looked at me but before she could speak I said: "Sorry I'm late Mom, but we had a great trip around the sheds."

I quickly went into detail, hoping to get in first before she told me off. It worked.

"Come on, sit down. Your tea's cold," she said.

"Thanks Mom. Looks great, I'll soon polish that off."

Dad came in and asked how the day had gone.

"Great, wanna see my numbers?"

I went off to bed thinking of all I had seen, and whatever it was that Melvin would bring me tomorrow - can't wait.

For a time, I sat looking at all the engine numbers I had collected but I soon noticed that some, well nearly half actually, consisted of only four digits. Besides these, we had seen some diesels and none of them were in my book so I would have to ask my mate Melvin about them.

THE FIELD OF PLEASURE

Arriving at school the next morning, I met up with the other two lads.

"Ok Al?," they asked.

"Yeah, great," I replied. "What a trip yesterday, eh? I've only just started to ease down. No wonder you lads are fit, all that running about, up and down them platform stairs."

They both smiled and then said together: "Here's Melvin."

We walked towards him and asked how he was.

"Fine," he said. "I've got an idea for Saturday."

He made no move towards his pockets as if to produce what he said he would bring me.

We entered the class and the teacher called off the register. I spent the morning thinking more about the next trip out and what plans Melvin could have for Saturday. More to the point, was I in those plans?

The day went rather fast and I set off for home at the usual time. I was not quite out of the playground when I heard Melvin call after me.

"That's for you," he said, handing me a Western Region locomotives book.

"It's a few months old but it contains the numbers from the shed we did yesterday. They're Western Region engines but it has Southern Region engines in it as well. Eastern Region engines and diesel books you'll have to get soon. Oh, and are you okay for a trip to Tamworth on Saturday?"

"Er, will ask Mom and Dad. Thanks for the book. I'll do a favour for you when I can. See ya tomorrow," I said in parting.

I scampered off home full of excitement, my mind now firmly on the weekend, plus all the new locomotive books I'm going to need and, more to the point, how to get them. Must do extra jobs for Mom and Dad, run a few errands for the neighbours. I reckon I need about a quid. No, more. There's the train fare to Tamworth, plus money for a good pad - this engine spotting is going to cost me a fortune.

It was Thursday evening - not much time to get jobs done. I needed a plan, and a good one - soon. I spent the evening running about the house cleaning up for Mom, helped Dad with a few jobs too. They never said much, only to tell me what jobs needed doing.

"Bed time," Mom said.

"Okay Mom. I'm just finishing putting my numbers in." I responded in the way that all kids that age did then and have done so ever since - always that little something extra to do to delay the inevitable march up the stairs.

"Did I show you my new Western book, Mom?" I asked.

"About ten times since you came home," she replied.

I was up very early the next day. Dad had gone off to work, Mom was doing the breakfast.

"Er, any jobs for me to do?" I enquired.

"No son, you did them all last night," said Mom.

"Oh, er yeah. Maybe some tonight then, eh?," I said.

"I'll see what I can find for you. Now get ready and off to school you go. Mustn't be late, it's Friday, last day before the weekend."

The weekend, yes. Hope to go with Melvin to Tamworth. Sounds great.

We all met up during the lunch break to talk over the Tamworth trip. The two lads were okay to go. I told Melvin I was alright to go but never did get round to asking Mom or Dad.

"This is the plan," explained Melvin.

"We will meet up at New Street early, say 7.30am. This will give us time to get the engines in the station before we catch the 8.10 to Tamworth."

The bell rang and I rushed off home with the hope of more jobs for me to do. My mom was getting ready to go out.

"Alex," she said. "I'm off into town for an hour or so, Dad will be home soon. He knows where I'm going."

Mom was still getting ready when Dad came in.

"Hello Dad," I called on hearing him come into the house.

"Okay son!," he shouted.

He hadn't got through the door when I asked if I could go to Town with Mom.

"Well, if your mom says its okay then, fine," he answered.

I found my mom's hat and asked if I could go with her. She looked across at Dad, he nodded.

"Come on then," she said. " And don't ask for anything. Short of money this week."

I thought to myself: "Everything's going wrong. No chance of the new books I need and no chance of Tamworth. I'll have to play this one by ear.

After tea, I washed and dried up for Mom. Dad, as usual, went out; he had arranged to meet up with Uncle Fred down the road at the Crown and Cushion. I spent most of the evening just messing about up and down the stairs, in and out of my bedroom.

"Alex, you're a real fidget tonight aren't you," said Mom.

"Yes Mom, sorry Mom," I said.

"Why don't you tell me what's wrong?"

"It's nothing, Mom," I said. "I'm okay."

It was Friday night and I was allowed to stop up late because there was no school tomorrow. All the jobs had been done and Saturday would be an easy day.

Dad arrived home just after 10.45. He was in his usual good and happy Friday night frame of mind.

"Got something for you," he said, pulling a paper bag out of the inside pocket of his suit.

"For me? Who from?," I asked.

"Fred thought you might need these," said Dad as he held out the bag.

Inside was a brand new ruler, half a dozen pens and a spanking new pad.

"Cor, thanks Dad. No. cor thanks Uncle Fred. Cor, thanks both of you."

I gave Dad a big hug.

He laughed and asked: "Where are you off to tomorrow?"

My excitement was very short-lived.

He chipped in again: "All this running around doing jobs, must be a reason."

"There is a reason, Dad, Mom. Melvin and the boys are off to Tamworth from early in the morning till just after teatime. They've asked me to go along with them," I explained.

"I have some money towards the train fare but not enough to cover it, and there's something else I really really need."

Dad and Mom looked at each other, waiting for one of them to speak. I chipped in quick: "Will do more jobs next week."

Dad asked me how much I needed.

"Well, just over a quid will cover it," I said.

"A quid, just to go to Tamworth for the day train spotting!" exclaimed my dad, clearly shocked by such extravagance.

"No Dad, I really need two more books, an Eastern one and a diesel one - plus a few bob to add to the train fare," I said, moving fast to defuse the situation.

"I'm at work early in the morning, doing some overtime till dinner time," he said. "What time do you want me to call you?"

"I'll get up with you Dad and travel into town with you till you get off the bus for work."

I raced upstairs to get my pens, books and pad all ready for the trip out. The night flew by and I heard Dad calling me. I was washed and ready in a flash, downstairs for breakfast, packed some sandwiches, sweets, pop, helped Dad with a few things and we were out and on to the bus. Dad paid the bus fares.

"Great," I thought. "Saved me a few coppers."

Just before Dad got off the bus he slipped me a quid, also an extra half-crown saying "Keep it to yourself." He put his finger to his lips, indicating to me to keep my mouth shut.

I waved to him as the bus pulled away, heading into town. It was nearly 7.20am and I was soon to meet up with the boys. My excitement grew as I anticipated the day ahead.

Off the bus in Union Street, a quick turn left and a short run towards New Street. I met up with the lads and our first job was to get a train ticket.

This time it never came from a bright red machine - must ask Melvin about that one at Snow Hill.

We collected the numbers off the trains that were in the station and then caught the 8.10 off platform 7. The engine was a Jubilee class loco and we strategically positioned ourselves in the very first compartment.

After about half an hour we were at Tamworth and, as usual, we followed Melvin. The reason for grabbing the first compartment became apparent. Once the train had arrived at Tamworh high level our carriage stopped dead opposite a gap in the station wall. Along with a number of other spotters, we nipped through the wall and scampered down a well worn bank. Then we ran over the spur line connecting the high and low level lines - making a mental note of the mogul loco that was stood there on pilot duty - then up another well worn grass bank, took an athletic skip over an old wire fence and joined all the others in the field of pleasure.

I soon realised that we were somewhere special - there must have been five or six hundred spotters in this field. Not only did trains pass alongside the field but they also passed just to our left on the main lines to London and the North. The railway above headed back to Birmingham and east to Derby, Sheffield and the North East. Melvin explained it all to me in between collecting our engine numbers.

In all the excitement, I'd forgotten to buy the new books that my dad had given me the money for, though Melvin said the shops on New Street station would still be open when we got back. Anyway, the chances of a Southern Region engine coming through Tamworth were very remote, he added with a wry smile. The chances of an Eastern Region engine coming through were also remote - Melvin had obviously been at this train spotting hobby for many years and knew his stuff.

I noticed after a while that the spotters all ran towards the fence just before a train went by, especially on the low level. Then they surged to the left of the field. Melvin noticed my looks of amazement at how they knew a train was coming, especially from the left on the low level where the view was completely obscured by the station.

"Look up at that tree," he said, pointing to a very large tree in the middle of the field. There was this lad perched about half way up.

"Now Alex, look at the other lad under the tree," said Melvin.

"Yes, I see him," I replied.

"That lad up the tree has a very powerful pair of binoculars and he can see the trains coming a long way off. He then tells his pal below who runs off and shouts 'There's a train coming' from whatever direction. He can even tell you the engine number before it gets here."

Tamworth became a great favourite of mine. We visited all the local places during the week but on Saturdays it was the place to be. Over the top were double-headed Scots, double-headed Jubilees, Black Fives, diesels, Peak namers, all sorts of different engines. On the low level were Coronations, Princesses, Britannias, Scots, Type 4 diesels, and the blue Deltic and prototype DP2 on trial.

We always followed the same routine until one day in 1962 - 7th July to be exact.

On this day we all piled off the train to find a British Railways official blocking the hole in the wall.

"Sorry boys," he stated. "There's no access to the field via your old route." He then continued: "Please make your way via the road. Oh, and no train spotting on the platforms."

Boos rained down on this poor unfortunate old lad. He was only doing his duty but our hobby was collecting loco numbers and in a strange way we felt it our duty to bunk through the opening in the wall.

Grudgingly, we all made our way via the main road to the field. On our approach we were met by some very disgruntled spotters. They were really annoyed.

Apparently, the farmer was not allowing spotters into his field. He gave no reason, one of his men just kept saying: "Sorry boys, no admittance today."

We hung around the road bridge for about an hour but many of the others left long before we did. We collected all the locos that passed underneath on the low level approach to Tamworth station but we could only hear the trains passing on the high level.

We made our way back to the station and were really surprised to find no-one on the high level platforms. A second or two later a voice called out: "Off the platform lads, unless you're catching your train home." We turned quickly and were confronted by a railway porter.

He looked somehow forlorn, an elderly lad; his uniform had seen better days. His cap was slightly tilted on one side and he made me smile as he trudged towards us. He walked as if the steps he was taking were his last.

He lifted his head up high and you could see how proud he once was of his job. Finally, he stood alongside Melvin, casually looking him up and down.

The porter's mouth opened and closed again. Then he spoke: "My, you're a big fella aren't yer."

Melvin, a little embarrassed and red in the face, only smiled politely.

The old lad then made us all laugh with his next comment: "You're a bloody great big lad, ain't ya." Even Melvin had to laugh at this. The old lad was chuckling to himself. He had us all in stitches when he said: "How bloody big are ya?"

All four of us were doubled up with laughter. My eyes and nose were running and my sides were aching. That great old chap really made our day.

We were still laughing when a train flew underneath on the low level. We all jumped up and just caught a glimpse of it flashing through the station on its way north.

Eventually we calmed down, my jacket sleeve was soggy with continuous wiping of my eyes and nose on it. It had seen better days anyway.

The old lad beckoned us towards the stairs and we followed. He then pointed over the wall towards some lads sitting on a fence near some mobile homes. It was the original spot where lads had gathered in the fifties, possibly before that. I'd heard stories about this place but I had never even thought about going there. Without another word he just walked away and disappeared into one of the rooms on the low level. We never saw him again.

We made our way into the small area and joined other lads who were sitting on a fence. We chatted about the closure of the field - no-one knew why.

Over the following weeks we made several more visits to Tamworth, nipped through the hole in the wall, down the bank, over the spur line and into the reopened field of endless pleasure.

We still visited sheds like Tyseley, Saltley, Aston and Monument Lane plus Snow Hill and New Street stations but we were by now starting to see the same locos over and over again. It was time to spread our wings.

Caught in the act but only by the camera of another enthusiast - a trio of lads just like us bunking Ardsley shed, West Yorkshire, in 1964. *(Photo by Arthur Chester)*

TASTING 'THE SMOKE'

It was well into 1961 and Melvin wanted to know if we could afford a trip to London.

This sounded great. I had never travelled that far before but I was only 12 and would have to ask Mom and Dad.

I arrived home doubly excited about Melvin's plan and thought for a while on who best to approach first, Mom or Dad, or both together. This was a tricky one. When they let me go with Melvin and the other lads there were never any problems and I was always home in good time. But London was a different matter, a very different matter.

"This is a trip further than any you have made before, Alex," my dad said.

"Yes Dad I know, but we're just seeing the same engines over and over again now," I explained.

"Yes, I know that," he said. "But we are only concerned about your welfare."

"I know Dad, but I'm with Melvin and the two other lads are going. I don't want to be left out, and I've a few bob saved up. Please Dad," I said, pleading my case.

"I'll let you know as soon as I come home from work tomorrow," he concluded.

"Cor, thanks Dad," I said gleefully as if my bid for London had already been accepted.

"I'm off to London," I kept muttering to myself, rubbing my hands and already getting my books, pens and pad ready.

"Great stuff, can't wait to give Melv the okay. The trip's on Sunday so all the engines will be on the sheds. Should be a trip to remember. Only a few days to go. Cor, great stuff."

Next day after school, Melvin and the lads were waiting in the payground for me. I hurried over to them with a great big smile on my face.

"So you're coming with us to London then," they said.

"My dad says he will let me know tonight when he comes home from work. Should be okay - has been in the past. My folks know we always stick together and that we look after each other."

The bell rang and I said "See ya tomorrow lads, must get off home and get some jobs done to raise extra dosh for London."

Arriving home, what a surprise, my uncle Fred was there.

"Hello Fred, great to see ya." I gave him a big hug. What timing Fred turning up just before my trip to London.

"By the way, Fred, thanks for those pens, also the ruler and pad. Just what I needed."

Fred just shook his head and smiled at me.

Fred had a very good job; he was in technical drawing somewhere in town and he was never short of a few bob. Now I had to really try and convince Fred that I needed a few bob for this trip to London, without appearing cheeky.

"Off to London on Sunday Alex, if Billy okays it?," he asked.

"Yeah Fred. How did you know I was off to London?," I enquired.

"Joan told me about your trips out collecting train numbers," Fred answered. "I've always believed that by travelling far and wide you get a better view of the world."

"I'm only going to London, Fred, not the other side of the world."

He laughed. "I know, I'm making a comparison."

"I know that, Fred. I'm making one of them as well."

We started to laugh again. Mom came in and asked what we were laughing at. This was a cue to laugh even more. Mom looked at us a bit offish and went back into the kitchen.

Fred said: "Whatever you do, don't upset your mom or you'll go nowhere."

He was right. I couldn't afford any problems at this stage. It was Friday tomorrow and I had to be on my best behaviour in the run-up to Sunday. This trip was too good to miss. I had to put Mom in a good frame of mind or I could kiss it all goodbye. Fred had another cuppa then said he would see Billy at eight down the Crown and Cushion.

"I'll see Fred out, Mom," I said.

I walked down to the bus stop with him and waited till the bus came. Just before it arrived he slipped me a ten bob note.

"Oh thanks, Fred. This will come in handy towards my trip."

The bus pulled away with Fred sat upstairs for a smoke. I waved till it was out of sight.

"Well done Fred," I said to myself. "Ten bob in my pocket plus a few bob I've saved up, plus a few bob off Dad. Mom might chip in. This could be the day of days, the trip of trips. Must get back, Dad's due home about now."

I was just arriving at the entrance to the maisonnette when I clocked Dad coming over the peck. I ran across to him.

"How's it going, Dad? How's work?," I asked.

"Fine, Son, everything's just fine," he answered.

"Any overtime tomorrow?," I enquired.

"No, nothing doing," said Dad.

"Uncle Fred's only just gone, about five minutes ago. He said he'll meet up with you at the Crown and Cushion about 8 o'clock," I said, continuing my build up to the big question.

"Right son, thanks. Now, about this trip you're going on - be okay?"

"Yeah, Dad. We are all going to stick together. We have always done so in the past and will continue to do so." I tried to sound reassuring.

"London's a big place, you know," he said.

"Yes Dad, but Melvin's been before and has it all planned out for the day."

"This lad, Melvin, he's okay you reckon?, he asked.

"Melv's great. He knows about the hobby and the places to go," I replied.

"That's it," I thought to myself. "I'm going, great stuff. Can't wait until tomorrow just to tell the lads I'm in for the trip.

Sunday morning came and I was up very early, not wanting to miss out by sleeping in, and to make sure I had packed everything I needed. I must have checked my bag a dozen times before I eventually went upstairs and said thanks and goodbye to Mom and Dad.

"Be careful, son," my Dad said.

"I'll be okay Dad," I reassured him

"Don't trouble with anyone, either," he added.

"No Dad. I'll keep with the lads all the time. Oh, and thanks for letting me go, also for the extra money."

"Dosh, you mean," said Dad with a smile.

"Yeah, thanks Dad."

The first bus up was a Midland Red. It cost a little bit more to travel on this service but it hardly stopped so I was into town early. I was the only person on the bus and sat downstairs next to the driver.

Church bells were ringing when I lept off the bus. Checking my watch, I saw it was just 9 o'clock and went to meet the others at Snow Hill station.

Our train was the 10 am to London Paddington, pulled by a King class loco and I 'copped' it.

"That's a great start to my day," I thought. "Hope the rest of it goes like this."

Melvin gave us all instructions on the route the train would take and pointed out all the depots along the way. We were to split up and go to the doorways of our carriage so we could get a better view of the locos on the sheds as we passed. This was a great system Melvin had devised and we missed very little on our way to Paddington.

The first depot we passed, on our right, was 84E Tyseley. We wrote down what we could see - the depot was a good distance from the main line but we got a few. Next came 84D Leamington Spa, just on our left, then 84C Banbury on the right.

"Time for some snap," Melvin suggested. "We won't see any more locos until we are closer to Old Oak Common. "

At Paddington station, we sat on the platform for a while, finishing our sandwiches and studiously examining the numbers we had got so far.

This was the biggest station I had ever seen. The other lads had been before but this was something to see. There were trains all over the place, you could taste the smoke, the smell of steam engines was unexplainable.

We whizzed about in all directions after all the locos and didn't miss any.

Melvin produced another book from his snap bag. "Right boys, follow me. Usual plan. Alex, you stick with me and just get the engines I send you for," he said.

"Right Melv. I've got the idea now, leave it with me."

We followed Melvin as he headed down the stairs to the Underground. He told us what ticket to get. Again, we followed without question, hopped aboard the tube and sped off to goodness knows where.

"This is it, boys, quick as we can," urged Melvin as the train slid into Willesden Junction station.

Crossing the road, we got round the nearby shed, 1A Willesden, in a flash.

"Hurry, boys," shouted Melvin as we ran down the road to Old Oak Common shed. It had four turntables and reminded me of Tyseley.

Running again, we caught a bus and found ourselves at 14D Neasden. After that, we had a short break while waiting for the bus to another shed, 14A Cricklewood.

There were engines everywhere we went and we got the lot, never missed one. Next was 1B Camden, then 14B Kentish Town. I was really warm by now but the day was to be a long one.

Then we arrived at the shed to see, 34A King's Cross. This was a shed where, for some reason, Melvin took his time about getting the numbers. He said to me as we went round: "Keep sharp, keep sharp."

Back outside the shed, we met up with the other lads. Melvin, looking at his watch, proclaimed: "Time for one more."

We got a bus outside King's Cross station and we seemed to be on it for ever. Still, it gave us the chance to have some snap and a drink. The journey was up when Melvin got out of his seat.

"Come on boys, must get a really fast move on at this one. No time to loose."

With Melvin leading, we stopped just outside an office set between two high walls. This was 70A, Nine Elms.

"Got a pass?," asked the foreman as he came out to see us.

"No sir," said Melvin in a sorrowful voice. "We've come a long way just to do your shed, but we will leave and not trouble you sir."

At this point Melvin began rubbing his eyes. The other lads looked down at the floor. Melvin sort of glimpsed at the foreman through slightly split fingers.

"Got it," I thought to myself. This was Melvin at his very best, a classic act of 'feel sorry for me mister.' The foreman must have felt bad, as he told us to hurry up but be careful, and report to him when we had got all the numbers.

"In." I thought. "We're in."

Out of the foreman's sight, we gave Melvin a great big hug for his Oscar-winning performance.

"That was brilliant, Melvin," I said.

"Yeah, real good of ya, Melvin, well played, Melvin," echoed the others.

The shed done, we were on our way back to Paddington.

"Thanks foreman, thanks for letting us in your shed, see you again, we hope," we chorussed at his office door.

"Bye lads," he said, waving us off out of sight.

Onto another bus and we arrived at Paddington with time for a quick run round the station collecting the engines that were there.

Eventually our train was in and we found a nice compartment and settled down to sort out our numbers before heading off home. Melvin told us about the other sheds we would pass en-route. There was 81C Southall, 81B Slough, Reading sub-shed down in the dip and 81D Reading, 81E Didcot, 81F Oxford, then Banbury again, though it could be dark by the time we reach Banbury.

The day was coming to an end, but as we passed the sheds in the dark, we still wrote down the numbers we could just about make out. Arriving at Snow Hill, I felt the day in London had just flown by. I never really had any time to stop and think. But that was the secret, there was no time to stop. The quicker you got round the sheds, the more locos you got.

Melvin had done us proud. He was the best in the business, he never gave up on any shed, ever.

We parted company, each going off in our different directions. I arrived home later than I wanted, my head still whizzing round at the speed with which the day had passed.

Mom and Dad were glad to see me, they wanted to know how my day had gone. My dinner was a bit baked from being kept warm in the oven but that was just how I liked it, the gravy all stuck round the edge of the plate and the roasters really well done. I licked my lips.

I never really had much time to reflect as after my meal I was straight off to bed - school in the morning.

Come Monday morning, school seemed the last thing on my mind but nevertheless I had to get up and make the effort, couldn't afford to show Mom and Dad that I couldn't make school because of the day in London.

MELVIN'S MASTERPIECE

Melvin had schemed up another of his classic plans, one that would, as always, be executed to perfection.

We were going to Crewe where we would visit all the sheds and, hopefully, be in good time to do the works as well.

It became something of a ritual, meeting up at New Street station around 10.30 on a Sunday morning for the 11.10 Glasgow train. Travelling north we would pass 21E Monument Lane or, if diverted because of engineering work, 21B Bescot. After Wolverhampton High Level came the Western depot at 84A Stafford Road and soon after, on our right, 21C Bushbury. The next shed was on our left at Stafford station. Approaching Crewe from the south, the long yard was always of interest with plenty of locos on the move then, just easing into Crewe, we passed 5B Crewe South. Into the station, pens writing down engine numbers as quick as they were seen we positioned ourselves strategically at the front of the train. This allowed us to be off the train as soon as it stopped, across the platform and over the footbridge into 5A Crewe North. First, we were round the straight shed, then very quickly into the semi-roundhouse which contained the big Coronation class Pacifics.

There was no time to gaze, we had to get on and mingle with the lads who were gathering outside the works entrance. They had permits to visit the locomotive works, we had Melvin.

There were two commissionaires on the gate, one checked your permit, the other watched you one by one enter a large gathering area. I think there were two parties leaving for two visits, one at 12.30 and the other at 2.30. Once everyone was inside the main gates, Melvin approached the commissionaire and asked, in his put-on lost soul voice, if the party organisers had left any permits going spare.

The commissionaire just answered: "No, sorry son."

This was the cue for Melvin to play his master stroke.

"Thankyou mister," he said in a sorrowful voice. Then he turned and looked at us waiting nearby. "Sorry lads, no permits today," he continued.

Our heads dropped. By then the party was moving away with one of the commissionaires in the lead.

Melvin reached into his pocket, pulled out a few bob, and said: "Well lads, looks like we'll have some cash left over for a pop and some sweets."

"I'd rather give the money to a good cause," said David. In those days the commissionaire would take a few bob off those lads he thought were okay.

"Come on, be quick about it," said the commissionaire, holding out a hand into which we in turn dropped our spare coppers. What he did with the money wasn't our business but there was a small tin just inside the office door for contributions.

The commissionaire shouted to his mate: "Hang on, some latecomers."

Some of the back marker boys in the party shouted towards the commissionaire who was well in front of the party to slow down, as others had arrived late. We hurried to join them, not wanting to cause any delay.

We tagged on the back of the party; some of the lads turned to us and said "Well done boys, glad you got in." Others just looked at us, laughed and stuck their thumbs up. They were all good lads that we saw on our spotting trips around the country.

The works was a real treat, locos being repaired, some lifted high up, freshly repainted engines gleaming inside the paint shop, and those outside often photographed by those who could afford a camera. We were just grateful to be in.

Afterwards, we thanked both commissionaires for seeing us round the works. We were at our best now, hoping that when we next tried to get in they would remember us being polite and friendly and let us in again. This, in fact, was the case on every occasion we visited them. It was another ploy of Melvin's: "Always be nice to these people and the shed foremen," he'd say.

The works done, we'd be off to the sub shed at Gresty Lane - a small shed with only a few locos on but they were from the Western Region so it was well worth popping into. Also, it was on our way to Crewe South. We bunked both these as fast as possible then sped back to the station for some well-earned snap.

Once again, we thanked Melvin for getting us round the sheds and especially the works. He took it all in his stride did our Melvin, never seemed to get flushed by any situation.

After spending a few hours on the station we caught a train back towards Birmingham, but we were by no means finished.

At Stafford, we were off and round the shed in a flash, then onto another train as far as Wolverhampton to do all the sheds there.

There were three sheds and a small works. The works was closed on Sunday but we could look through the windows and get most of the numbers. I said, as I always did: "They should clean these windows more often."

After the works, we followed the canal to Stafford Road and then 84B Oxley. The money still holding out, we could get a bus to Bushbury and then it was home time.

Arriving back at New Street, it was a quick "tarrar" to the lads and onto the bus home for my Sunday dinner. I could smell it on entering the house and boy was I always ready for it.

The folks were glad to see me home safe.

"Enjoy the day out at Crewe?," Dad asked. He looked into my book and smiled at the amount of locos we had seen.

"I do enjoy this hobby," I said. "The travelling can only be good for my education. I'm learning about the places I visit and about various parts of the country - it's helping me in a geographical way."

Mom raised her eyebrows and looked at Dad. They were far from daft. They knew me and how I operated, but played along.

Time for bed. Winter nights and winter weather have now taken a grip on the country. Can't really say how many more trips I will be able to make.

The freezing weather was taking its toll. Everything was being affected, trains included and we all felt that a break from our trips was a wise move. We could not afford to get stuck anywhere.

My Christmas list was full of new books that I wanted, especially train timetables. They were a bit like the loco books, one for each region and the cost was about the same, 2/6d. The colours were also the colours of the regions - the London Midland was reddish, the Western a browny-beige, the Eastern Region was blue and the Southern Region green. The other books I wanted were a Locoshed book giving the depot allocations of all the locomotives, and the book which Melvin used on all our trips - the Shed Directory.

Crewe works must not be missed under any circumstances. Apart from the sheer quantity of engines always in for overhaul, they came from a wide area and we were always guarenteed plenty of cops. *(Photo on 23rd June, 1962 by Peter Wood)*

A RISKY RIDE

Christmas passed, New Year came trailing by and we were into 1962. The weather was bad and the talk was worse to come. I had hoped to get together with Melvin and David but Mom and Dad made it quite clear that this was not the sort of weather to be out and about in.

The holidays over, we were back to school - our school never closed. Melvin and David were just like me, itching to get out on a trip. Every day the conditions were improving and, finally, we got so fed up that we went on a local trip to Rugby, bunked the shed and spent the rest of the day near the bridge where the Great Central line passed over the top.

I noticed a long line of Patriot class locos with rags tied over their chimneys. I also noticed how Melvin's face dropped as we walked past them writing down the numbers. A look of sadness had taken hold of this usually cheerful face. I didn't ask him why the sad look but something must have hit home for this to happen. In all the time I had spent in his company, I had never seen such an expression.

The weeks that followed were spent planning future trips though at weekends we still took in depots closer to home. London was on our list again, plus another run up to Crewe.

Derby was the next visit. This was a new depot for me, and the works were just nextdoor so we did them as well. Then Melvin suggested we push our luck and catch a train to Stoke. I suggested we got tickets to Crewe and then went home via Stafford so we pooled our dosh but there wasn't enough for that.

We headed out of the freezing cold and into the waiting room, and a welcome warm place it was too. We joined the other people waiting for their trains and, moving as close as we could to the fire, began eating our sandwiches, drinking our pop, and then the biscuits or cake, always eaten last, like a treat after teatime. I'd hardly tucked into my egg sarny when Melvin shouted, a little on the loud side: "Stuff this, come on boys, let's go!"

With bits of egg and bread crumbs spilling from my mouth onto the waiting room floor, I scrambled to get my snap, bag and books together. David was all hands reaching for everything.

We followed Melvin towards a local train waiting in the bay platform.

"Hold up, Melvin," I cried. "My sandwiches have fallen out my bag!"

David was still totally in a mess clutching all his bits and bobs while struggling to catch us up.

Once again, I called to Melvin to slow down. He turned to me saying: "Get a stride on or we'll miss the train" and disappeared into the train in the bay platform. Then, his head popped out of a doorway. "Come on lads, this is the one."

David and I quickened our pace, jumped through an open carriage door, and then the train guard appeared.

I looked over in David's direction. He was still scoffing part of his sandwich. Bread crumbs all round his mouth, he asked me: "Where are we going?"

I shrugged my shoulders and answered: "Don't know, Melvin's gone off talking to the guard."

Melvin reappeared with the guard in company.

"Okay lads?,", the guard asked us.

"Yes," we answered together.

"Loco snatching are you?," he continued.

"Yes, I've never been before," David answered.

"Nor me," I said.

"Did you have a pass?" the guard asked.

This time neither David nor I said anything. There was a short pause then the guard started to laugh. Melvin started to laugh, but David and I were not in on whatever was going on between them.

The train started to slow down. The guard turned away, laughing, and headed in the opposite direction. Once he was out of sight and earshot, David asked Melvin if everything was okay.

"Yes," replied Melvin. "The guard's an old wagger."

"A wagger, what's a wagger?"

David laughed. I looked at him and said: "Don't you start this laughing lark off again."

"Right, right," Melvin chipped in. "He's an old loco spotter just like us."

The guard reappeared and spoke to us about the times when he used to travel far and wide collecting loco numbers, but just as the story became interesting he went off again as the train slowed down. After a few stations, he said sorry about the questions but he was just playing us up.

David said he knew that. I admitted I thought he was serious.

The stories continued and we sat there taking it all in.

A tinge of excitement came into the guard's words as he took us off in the direction of his compartment. Opening a window, he pointed at another shed on our right.

"Look, there's 16A Nottingham Midland," he said.

We immediately wrote down what numbers we could see. David moved quickly to another window, trying to get down as many locos as possible. The guard called a few off. I was writing and listening at the same time and got a bit confused but I knew he was only trying to help.

We arrived in Nottingham. Melvin took it all very calmly. Me, I'd never been here before and I felt a bit bewildered.

The guard was met by another guard. They exchanged a few words and the other guard climbed aboard and disappeared into his compartment. The guard we were with told us to meet him outside the front of the station. We looked at each other and, shrugging our shoulders, walked out to the entrance and waited.

We were a bit concerned about waiting for a person who had shown a lot of interest in us. I asked Melvin if it would be an idea to scarper.

David chipped in: "We never paid the train fare, either. How are we going to get back to Derby?"

Melvin, now in deep thought, was just about to answer our questions when we were startled by the honking of a car horn.

"Jump in, lads," called the guard. "Hurry up, jump in."

David and I slowly eased our way into the back. Melvin got in the front.

We never spoke a word as the car moved away from the station entrance. I was a bit scared, not knowing what situation we may have allowed ourselves to get into. You never know.

The guard then, for his own reasons, reassured us we were in for a surprise. He kept on driving until we left the city and headed out into the countryside. Melvin stared out of the windows, trying to follow the road signs and work out where we were going. Surely, the guard must know from our silence that we felt uncomfortable in a car with someone we had only just met an hour ago.

"Nearly there," he said.

"Nearly where?," asked Melvin.

"You'll see," he said, smiling as if to put us at ease. We had arrived.

"Do you know where you are lads?," he asked us.

I never answered, neither did David. Melvin also remained quiet.

"None of you been to this depot?,"

I answered no. David, shaking his head, also answered no, but Melvin said: "I think I came here a few years ago."

"It's 16B," the guard said. "The depot is Kirkby-in-Ashfield."

"Yes, I've been here before," said Melvin. "The bus stop back towards Nottingham is just around the corner. I think there's a little shop nearby."

The guard said: "That's right but its a little further up the road from the bus stop."

As we eased our way out of the car, the guard said: "I live about half a mile from here."

We all thanked him for the trip from Derby and for the stories he had told us on the way.

"Any time, boys," he said. He waved, and was gone.

With no time to loose, we scurried round the shed very quietly - we didn't wish to make our presence known. The numbers down, we were out and away.

The Shed Directory in Melvin's hands, we now awaited our next move. Melvin was studying this book when a bus approached. We put our hands out and it stopped. Melvin apologised to the driver and asked for directions to another depot he thought might be quite close.

"Jump in lads." We did as Melvin said.

Melvin was again in deep discussion with the driver who was very helpful. He reported back: "We're off to another depot that's on our way back to Nottingham. It's 16D Annesley."

The driver called Melvin to join him. Trying to tidy up his bag, Melvin went to see what the bus driver wanted. He seemed to be a long time. Eventually he returned, explaining that the driver had given him directions.

"Great," I said. "But we haven't paid any fare yet, Mel."

"Oh, right, I'll go and ask how much we owe him," said Melvin.

"All taken care of," he said, returning with a cheeky smile on his face. David looked at me.

"Yes," I thought, "All taken care of."

"Right boys," the driver shouted. "We're here."

We each said our thanks as one by one we climbed off the bus. He waved, beeped the horn and moved off out of sight.

"Let's hurry lads," shouted Melvin. "We must get a stride on."

Again, we were in and out of the depot with speed and silence, that was our trade mark.

We were now feeling very pleased with ourselves. Melvin, looking at his watch and then up to the sky, agreed that we had anough time to get another depot in. We boarded another bus, the destination indicating that we were heading back towards Nottingham. Once there, we hurried around looking for another bus to take us to 40E Colwick.

The driver put us off and, again with speed, we were just about to enter the shed when a voice rang out: "Where are you lot going?"

We stopped in our stride. Melvin, as quick as lightening, answered: "We're looking for the shed foreman."

A rather large man appeared. "I'm the shed foreman. Have you a permit?," he snapped.

"No, sorry sir," came the reply from Melvin. We turned to walk away when Melvin gave another classic "feel sorry for me" look.

"Sorry mister," he said again. "But we were honestly looking for the foreman. Come on lads, it's a long way home to Birmingham." The word Birmingham spoken loud.

We made our way out of the entrance and very, very slowly moved off. I felt my legs going at the speed of a tortoise. David began rubbing his eyes. We never turned around, we just hoped that the foreman would be watching us, feel sorry for us and call us back. Well, that was our usual ploy but this time it didn't work.

We were about four or five yards from the depot when a voice called out to us. We slowly turned to find we were being approached by a railwayman. He gave us a piece of paper with the numbers of all the locos on it.

Melvin thanked him and opened the piece of paper and right enough there were the numbers of all the locos on the shed. But the rule was that you must see the locos.

"Back to the shed lads, we'll try another plan," said Melvin.

We hurried back to the foreman's office. Melvin approached him and a cheerful smile came across his face. The foreman was surprised to see us again. Melvin thanked him for giving us the numbers.

"That's okay," he said. "That's okay."

Melvin then set about explaining how the hobby worked, that we had to see the locos before they counted. He showed the foreman all the Nottingham sheds we had visited and told him how nice and friendly the other shed foremen had been.

The Colwick foreman held up his right hand and said: "Alright, I've heard enough."

Melvin chipped in saying: "You're a nice foreman for taking the time to write the numbers down for us."

The foreman looked straight at Melvin, paused for a moment, then asked Melvin if he acted like this with every foreman who wouldn't let us round his depot.

"You've got me there," Melvin replied. We all smiled about the fact that our Melvin had won again.

The foreman smiled at us and said: "Come on."

We followed him to another small room. He called to one of the railwaymen to show us round the shed.

"Great," we said, thanking him.

"Off you go but be careful, and report back after," he said.

The engine driver took us all round the shed and took great pride in telling us about the different locos and the work they did in the area. We were trying to hurry as fast as possible because time was getting on but we still took a deep interest in what he was saying. The shed done, we paid him our thanks and he took us back to the foreman.

"Okay boys? I hope you enjoyed the tour of the shed," asked the foreman.

"Cor, yeah, thanks gaffer, thanks a lot," we said, bidding him goodbye.

We boarded another bus and headed back towards Nottingham with just enough time for one last depot, close by the station. This was 16A, the shed we passed on our way into Nottingham. It was a fair walk so we put our feet down and trotted to the shed. We half looked for the foreman, writing the numbers down as well. We were soon finished and out.

Back at the station our first task was to find out about our train home. The time was now 5.15pm. It had been a long day but we were all very pleased with the sheds we had got into. The train was at about 5.45 which gave us enough time for some snap. We had been so busy running around we hand't had any since Derby - and that was only a nibble.

"We have a small problem boys," Melvin stated.

"What's that?," David asked.

"The money's a little short, and we never paid any train fare from Derby to here. All our money has gone on bus fares to get us round the sheds."

As usual, Melvin was right.

"Let's go and see the guard and say that we were collecting loco numbers at Derby when we met up with some boys from somewhere near and, er no, forget that," I said.

"Christ," I went on, "We do need an answer to this one." I looked over in Melvin's direction. David also looked at Melvin.

"We'll tell the guard the truth," Melvin declared.

"What? We're done for," I said. "He won't believe that for a minute. He'll just say we're making it up."

David piped up: "No. maybe Mel's got the answer. If this guard knows the other guard he may believe us."

"Yes," I said, "That's all very well but what if he doesn't know him, the truth won't be of any real importance then."

"We have as much chance with that idea as with any other we're going to come up with," said David.

"Err, look," said Melvin, "Let's just see what happens. The guard may not come round. We've been very lucky today, our luck might just hold out."

"Okay, let's hope so," I said.

The train was announced and we got on board with fingers crossed.

"It's no good lads," Melvin said. "Let's go and see the guard and tell him what happened and why our dosh is short. At least we've told the truth. You never know, it may prove a wise move."

David and I had to agree. We went off in search of the guard and we had-n't got a few yards when we saw him heading in our direction, asking for tickets as he moved closer and closer towards us. Finally we met up. Melvin was about to explain when the guard turned and walked away. The train slowed down and then stopped. We carried on after the guard and as we did the train started to move off again.

Again we met up with the guard and Melvin began to explain that we had a small problem with our tickets. He was just about to go into more detail when the guard suggested we wait for him to do the tickets after which he would come back to us. He pointed towards his compartment; we skulked off in that direction and waited. After a while, the guard reappeared, sat himself down and asked for one of us to explain why none of us had any tickets.

Melvin took his cue to inform the guard of the very details that we all hoped he'd believe. After listening to the tail, he gave Melvin a piece of paper and asked us all to write down our names and addresses. We did this in front of him, we had nothing to hide.

He asked us again to describe the guard on the other train. Melvin described him to a tee.

"A red car, you said the other guard had?," the present guard asked.

"No. no. It was a darkish blue, I'm sure," David said.

"Okay," the guard said. "Give me the paper."

"I've not written my address on it yet," I said.

"You don't need to," replied the guard. "You're not lying. I know that guard he lives out at..." he paused for a moment.

Melvin was in as quick as a flash.

"He lives at Kirkby-in-Ashfield, near the loco shed."

The guard ripped the paper up and scattered the bits out of the window.

"Okay boys, off you go. Get a seat at the front."

The train pulled into Derby station and we hurried away to seek our last train home to Birmingham. It was now very dark. Melvin soon found the timetable, calling our attention to the train time and the platform. We sat and reflected on another great day out, all the sheds we had visited, all the locos we had seen and how many cops we'd got.

We jumped on the train, found a good, warm compartment, got our books out, and some more snap and pop.

"We're off," I said. "Home time."

It was well after 8pm when we got back to Birmingham, a very long day but more than worth the effort.

When I got home, Uncle Fred was there.

"Hello Fred. Hello Mom, Dad. Great to see ya. Great to be home. Wow, what a day we've had. You should see my loco pad full of sheds, new ones at that, locos all over the place. I must have copped a stack, plus five new sheds today."

Mom said: "Calm down, calm down. I'll get your tea warmed up."

"Thanks Mom, thanks a lot." I looked forward to my supper always well done, just how I liked it.

I soon scoffed that up, had a drink and then went off to bed.

"Must get up early and help with a few jobs, need the dosh for next week-end," I thought to myself.

I had a quick wash and got into bed, thinking about the day over and over again.

Mom called me down: "Not saying goodnight then?," she asked.

"Sorry Mom, Dad, Fred, so excited."

Fred passed me a small brown container.

"Open it in the morning, promise?," said Fred.

"Oh yeah I will. Thanks Fred," I said.

"And here is something for your next trip." He handed me half a crown.

Arriving home after school on Monday, my first task was to arrange the teatime plates, clear away any rubbish, do some tidying up - loads of jobs before I could set too marking up my numbers from yesterday. And there was that present from Fred.

Quickly, I whizzed about the house, looking for anything to do before Mom and Dad arrived home. The more jobs I did, the more I found to do and the better for me money-wise. The further the trip, the more dosh I would need.

I was just about to open Fred's present when Mom came in from work, closely followed by my dad. The time spent house cleaning had gone faster than I thought. No time to open Uncle Fred's present now, must help Mom with the tea then it'll be wash up, dry up and put all the crocks away.

Tea over, jobs done, now upstairs to my loco books and a quiet hour putting my numbers in.

"Have you opened the present from Fred yet?," Dad asked.

"No dad, not really had the time." I was still going through the numbers from our trip to Derby and Nottingham.

"Leave that for a while," he said. "Look at what Fred's bought you"

I hurried back upstairs for the brown container. Feeling at it, I tried to guess what it was. Back downstairs, I opened it.

"Look at this!," I shouted, taking out a black Brownie 127 camera. "Look at this!," I shouted again, holding it up to show them.

"Don't drop it," Mom said. "There's a film inside it."

Dad looked over at Mom, then said "Yes, be careful. They aren't too strong, those cameras."

"All this from Fred, he must really like me," I said to Mom and Dad.

"Yes," Dad said, "Plus the half crown."

"Oh yeah, I'd forgotten about that."

I asked Mom how many pictures were on a film roll.

She thought for a while. "I think there's twelve on that one. When you take it in to be developed you had better remember to ask them. Or after twelve, see if it goes any further, but take it steady."

I was really excited by now, thinking to myself: "A new camera, film in it, 2/6d in my pocket. What a good start to the week this had been.

THE RAILWAY ENTHUSIAST

I decided to take my camera round Saltley and Aston sheds after school. This way I could get out and about for a few hours and get into the swing of taking photos. I dashed home from school, grabbed my books, pens, pad and camera and set off walking, to save money. The light nights now gave me more time for my hobby.

I arrived at Saltley about teatime and began scampering round the shed - had to get a move on because there was still Aston to do. I was just about to take my first ever photo when I felt a hand on my left shoulder.

Slowly turning, I discovered I had been collared by an engine driver. He looked down on me, said nothing at first, there was just a long pause. Then he pointed towards a row of Royal Scot class locomotives.

"Take a photo of those," he said, still pointing towards the line of Scots.

I focussed on 46132, noticing the nameplate was missing.

"Turn that white knob," he said. "No, the other way. Here, let me show you."

He took the camera and showed me in which direction I should turn the knob. The film inside turned very gently round.

"Look," he said. "Number two."

"Oh, right, got it now," I said.

He began to show me about taking photos at different angles and from a variety of positions. I would, he said, get better results. I thanked him, then he walked me out.

I had only walked a few yards away when I turned and called back to him. He stopped, pointed his finger to his chest, a gesture to ask if it was him I was calling to.

"Yes," I nodded my head. "Wait a tick. Can I ask you a question?"

"A question, about what?," he asked.

"Those locos, the Scots," I said. "Why are there no nameplates on them?"

He took my book of numbers and pointed to the list that ran down the page.

"Those are on their way to Carlisle within the next few weeks. After that they are due for cutting up. I looked down the list and felt something hurt inside me. The list looked very impressive, all eight of these locos lined up: 46162, 46160, 46122, 46103, 46132, 46137, 46123 and 46157.

He looked down at me. My face was how I remember Melvin's at Rugby. I recalled that time, when he never said a word - the look on his face was words enough.

"Yes, son," the driver said. I knew what he meant. For a moment he stared down at the concrete floor, a look of sadness across his face.

He turned and walked slowly away. Could he be sharing the same feelings as me, and as Melvin at Rugby?

I watched him go out of sight then got myself together. "Must get a move on, Aston next," I reminded myself.

My pace quickened and the thoughts of a few seconds ago were soon gone. I geed myself up by thinking of what might be on Aston shed and what photos I would take.

It was after six when I arrived at the shed and there was trouble in the air. A few spotters were stood outside the foreman's office in Longacre Road and some shouting was going on. As I got nearer to the shed, I could make out some engine drivers close to the foreman's office. They were telling these lads off for some reason. I never got the facts but kept on walking away and turned left into Holborn Hill. I climbed up the wall just to see what I could but thought twice about bunking the shed.

I sat looking at the locos for a while, still considering whether I should try and bunk the shed or let it go under the circumstances. It would have been the first time I had passed up a shed since taking up this hobby.

"Let it go Alex," I said to myself. "Never know what's happened and what trouble you may walk into." Climbing down, I made my way down the hill and away from the depot.

I must admit I was a bit annoyed at not only missing out on the shed but also the photos I could have got. I resolved to keep it to myself about missing Aston. There was no written rule on loco spotting but we never came away from our trips having missed a shed. No matter what the problem, a way in would be found, so dedicated were we to this hobby.

I pondered over what might have happend. "Was there a problem inside the shed? Had someone been hurt while they were in there? Must be a reason." I could think of nothing else all the way home.

It was coming up to 8 o'clock when I got back to our maisonnette. Mom and Dad were watching TV. I didn't feel like doing anything, just ate my tea, said goodnight and went off to bed. I spent a short time looking at the locos I'd seen on Saltley, put the cops into my book and fell asleep.

My mom was very quiet the next morning and when I finally came down for breakfast she took a long time to speak to me. I sensed that something was wrong. I waited for her to make the first move but as it got nearer to school time I felt I had to ask if there was a problem.

"Mom, er you and Dad okay?", I asked, nervously.

She turned and looked at me, a half smile came across her face.

"Yes," she answered. "We're okay, why?,"

"I just thought that something was wrong, that's all," I said.

"No son, everything's fine. We thought that there was something wrong with you, though," she said.

I explained about the touble at Aston which had been playing on my mind.

"It's passed now," she said.

"Mom's right," I thought to myself. "Forget it. I'm off to school to see the lads, see what's happening. That's more important than what happened yesterday."

I arrived in good time to see a sight worth seeing and to hear words worth hearing. The playground was, as usual, a buzz of different sounds, sometimes so noisy you couldn't hear yourself talking to someone very close to you. At times, you had to shout to be heard.

Melvin marched into the centre of the playground. He was clutching a book of some sort, partly hidden by his hand and held close to his chest. He paused for a moment then, standing upright like a guardsman on parade with his chest sticking out, he announced: "I am no longer a train spotter."

People nearby were stopped in their tracks as Melvin began his speach. David and I looked at each other. We turned and focussed on him. A silence fell around where he stood clutching the book like Moses with the Ten Commandments. Time seemed to stand still. Then, with his right hand, he took the book and held it aloft proclaiming: "I am now a railway enthusiast!"

Swearing rained down on Melvin. His announcement was an open invitation to all sorts of abuse. Wise cracks were coming thick and fast in poor Melvin's direction.

"Your a ....so and so. You silly old ..... Stick it up your ....." The sarky comments continued for quite some time. Even David and I had to laugh. Melvin's face, completely straight and serious to this point, began to crack as he too dissolved into laughter. As always, he took it all in his stride.

Melvin was still laughing when people began clammering to look at his new book. Others tapped him on the shoulder saying: "Well said Melv, you do make us laugh" or "Stand up for yourself," others shouted, "Let's see your book." He had again won them all over with his timing and the way he could deal with any situation.

David and I apologised for laughing and made it clear we were not laughing at Melvin but at the comments made by others. He was still smiling when he asked: "Wanna see my new book?"

We only got into the first few pages when the bell rang and Melvin took the book back.

"In the break," he said. "Look at it in the break."

We joined the other lads and went into class.

Melvin's new book was an Ian Allan combined volume. Hard bound, it was full of all the regions' locomotives, all the shed codes, diesels and electrics, plus loads of different photos, in fact everything except the Shed Directory.

Melvin was now indeed a "railway enthusiast."

THE WORKS PARTY

We were still taking in Tamworth on Saturdays and watching diverted trains come through Perry Bar on Sundays while I made a few local trips to take some more photos.

I was enjoying this new side to my hobby and told Melvin and David about the camera. They thought it a good idea to take photos so long as we were not pushed to get round the sheds.

Getting the locos was far more important than photos. At the time, that seemed right. You had to stop, get the camera out, set up the photo, the other two would have to look out for anyone coming - it all cost precious minutes.

By now we were again starting to get fed up with staying local at weekends and Melvin suggested another trip to London, just to do the main sheds. We agreed and so, off we went on Sunday 1st July, 1962.

Old Oak Common was packed with locos, Nine Elms too, King's Cross had eleven A4s on. We also saw a wide variety of diesels, especially at Old Oak and King's Cross. There were only a few at Nine Elms but two were Warships. It was a good day and the light nights meant we could see more on our journey home.

After running errands for anyone on the block, for Mom, and Dad, I had by now saved up a lot of money, and I would need it as Melvin was not going on holiday this year which meant extra trips in the summer hols.

A trip to Doncaster was planned for Sunday, 22nd July, 1962 and a great day out it turned out to be. I filled a whole page just on the way. En-route we passed Saltley, Burton, Derby, Hasland and just before we reached Sheffield, on our left hand side, was 41C Millhouses.

The train had not been stopped for a second when we were running as fast as we could out of Sheffield Midland station, turning right and following Melvin up towards Sheffield Victoria. The long slope up to Victoria station took all the energy out of us but we had to keep going. The train times were very tight and if we missed this one there would be a long wait for the next.

We made it just as the guard was giving the driver the signal to go. We got our breath back and looked out for the Tommy locos.

Then, suddenly, there were two together, then another two.

"Great stuff," I thought, copped all four. Well, it was my first sighting of these electrics.

Melvin called us over. "Keep a sharp lookout over there." He pointed to a depot coming up on our right. It's 41A Sheffield Darnall," he told us.

We wrote the numbers down as soon as they were in close view.

"Stacks there," I said. We always split up when approaching a shed - more space to see and write.

The train soon arrived at another place that I had never been to. Just as we turned the curve into Mexborough station, the shed was on our right. Again, we clammered for the best view - there looked to be a few on. Sunday was a reasonably quiet day on any part of the railway system so there were more locos at the sheds.

We were in luck. I spotted a couple of lads boarding our train just as it was about to pull out. I headed in their direction.

"Okay lads?," I asked them. "Did you get into the shed?"

"Yes," came the reply. "You want the numbers?," one of them asked.

"Oh yeah, thanks," I replied.

When you approached the station, you could see along the lines of locos and even see inside the shed but you couldn't see all the numbers so it was really useful if you could get the numbers from someone else who had been round the shed already. This is how we worked, all helping each other; that way we never missed many locos.

Doncaster station looked something special. As we turned left from the Sheffield line we saw a few locos stood there, one was sparkling in the sunshine, just out of the works, others looked just the opposite, waiting to go in.

The train came to a stand. The two lads that we had met were off like a shot.

"Hurry up!," they called to us. "The works, the works, come on!"

We chased after them, trying not to loose sight of them.

"The works party, just like Crewe," Melvin said. Our speed increased as we tried to stay close to our new friends.

We trailed the two lads down the stairs, under the subway and up another flight of stairs to be confronted by the ticket collector.

"Tickets please, tickets please," he said.

"We're all together," we replied and one by one we hurried passed him, giving him no time to clip our tickets, a quick glance was all he was going to get. I was the last one to pass him.

"What's all the rush?," he asked me.

"The party," I answered, "the works party."

I followed the lads through the car park. Melvin was in third place, and then David. We turned right over a railway bridge and right again, dipping down towards what I thought was the works entrance but the two lads at the front swerved left and kept running as if life itself depended on them getting there in time. The commissionaire was closing the gates just as we ran up to them.

"The party's gone," he said. "They've all gone." The lad at the front swore with his last breath.

41

All five of us were bent over trying to catch our breath after what must have been a five or six-minute dash from getting off the train to reaching the works entrance. No one spoke for a while, as if we were waiting for someone to make the first sensible suggestion.

"I'm not giving up," Melvin said. "I know this place and how to get in. Anyone with me?"

The two lads looked at Melvin in a very inquisitive way. Oh yes, Melvin had been there before.

When we got our breath back the other two decided they would go to the shed. They said "See ya" and began walking away.

I suggested that Melvin called them back so that they could bunk the works with us but Melvin said that while three of us had a chance of sneaking in, five would make it much more difficult. I agreed.

We were soon running alongside a high wooden wall, peeping through the cracks now and then to see if any locos were there. It seemed to go on forever but we were motivated by the thought of what might be at the end. Finally, we came to the end, and could see a couple of locos at the back of the works - 70036 Boadicea and 61151.

We scrambled through some shrubs, some wire and across a bit of waste ground, never looking back. We got behind the works and hid behind some oil drums, peeping over the top just to make sure we hadn't been spotted.

"So far so good," whispered Melvin. I was shaking with fright but tried not to show it. Melvin told us to stay put while he checked the side door to the works building.

"This is the plan," he said, looking down at his watch. "I reckon that if the party walks down the near side first it should be close by within the next six or seven minutes. If they walk the far side then it could take up to 15.

"Can't hide here for that long, certainly not 15 minutes," I thought to myself. "We could get copped and that's trouble for us all."

I said: "Look Melv, why don't we just ease our way inside, keep out of sight then at the right moment just slip into the party as it comes by. If anything goes wrong we can say we had drifted away from the party."

Melvin thought then said : "Okay."

"Shush," I said, "Someone's coming, shusshh."

We ducked down behind the oil drums.

"Quick," said Melvin, "let's get further back. Over there." He pointed. "Hurry Alex."

The party had made its way out of the works to collect the few locos standing in the yard. My heart was beating like a machine gun, all sorts of silly things were going through my head. What if we get caught - the police, Mom, Dad?

The commissionaire led the party out of the side door and they passed us one by one. There must have been 50 or 60 of them, some were taking photos, others talking and writing down the numbers.

With his right hand and then his left hand, Melvin indicated for us to stand up and make out we were with the party. His hands were flapping up and down, like a bird trying to take off. We all stood up at the same time and made out we were looking up at the tall works building while talking to each other. My heart was in my mouth, and my mouth was dry as a bone.

I could not have spoken a word if my life depended on it. Melvin, on the other hand, was quite calm, as if he was the party leader, pointing here, there - all part of the act.

As the party made its way back into the works we edged our way slowly into the group, Melvin made a point of talking to someone, to make anyone who might be a bit wary of us feel as though we had been with the party from the start.

We entered the huge building and I felt myself starting to ease down for the first time since we started running from the station. That seemed hours and hours ago but it was only three quarters of an hour since. We strolled round the works writing down every single number. There were a few diesels in for repair, plus the steamers. The highlight was No. 60009 Union of South Africa, an A4 Pacific. It was up in the air - the whole of the locomotive suspended from a great overhead crane. I had never seen anything like it.

The party went through another door and out into the daylight. The commissionaire led it to the gate where it had first come in and that was the end of the tour.

We may have missed a couple of locos but not to worry, we saw a lot more than we missed and it had been a real treat.

Melvin, who had stayed away from David and me during the latter part of the tour rejoined us as we got out of the works.

"I've got all the information about the shed," he told us excitedly.

No time to lose, we were now on our way to the shed, 36A. We started to trot, then it became more of a quick stride and soon we were into a run until we reached the edge of the depot.

Melvin gave us our instructions: "Alex, front yard. David, back yard and the little maintenance shop. I'll do the shed. Oh, and by the way, according to one of the lads at the works, there are over 160 locos on shed so we must speed up."

We parted and covered the whole of the area that Melvin had told us to. Once round the shed, we returned to the station for our train home.

"Have we got time for some snap?," asked David.

"Oh, if you have to," laughed Melvin

In an instant David looked a real picture, his mouth half full of corn dog, crumbs all round his face, even on his nose. He was messy at times but his eating habits made us laugh.

I tucked into my favourite egg sandwiches and Melvin his Spam sandwiches, a nice swig of pop to wash them down and then a couple of Jammie Dodgers.

We were well pleased with the day so far. His face now cleared, David spoke up: "Nearly 250 so far and we still have the journey home. Five Deltics, three A4s, four Brits, not bad eh?"

"Don't forget the Tommy locos, there were four of them," I quipped.

The train rattled its way towards Sheffield. On the way we passed Mexborough again, then Darnall before arriving back at Sheffield Victoria. We ran back down towards Midland station - it was much easier than coming up, our feet seemed to fly down the ramp.

We climbed aboard the Birmingham train and settled into a single compartment, got out our books and started checking all the numbers from our trip so far.

Melvin had his head out of the window; he was muttering about 'the lady.'

"I bet she's at the front," he muttered to himself.

"Yes, yes, I can see her," he said to us. "Just as I thought, she's right down the front. I'm not going all the way down there," he moaned.

David started to laugh. He placed his left hand at the side of his mouth and said quietly: "The char lady."

"Oh yeah," I said.

"No, no, no, again," Melvin said to himself, his head still out of the window. "I'm not going to chase after her." He pulled his head in.

The engine whistled and the train slowly began to ease out of the station. Melvin stared speechless at the window as we passed the char lady. Then he snapped: "Come on, let's take a peep at Millhouses."

Char ladies could be seen with their refreshment trollies at all the big stations where expresses called as few trains had their own catering facilities then. This one turned out to be of no use to us and Melvin had to stay hungry and thirsty.

After passing the next shed, Hasland, I opened my bag and, just to tease Melvin, slowly brought out another few Jammie Dodgers.

He glanced out of the corner of his eye, then looked back at his loco numbers.

I was just about to slip it into my mouth when he again, rather casually, glanced towards the biscuit.

"No," I said loudly, "I'll save them for later," and moved to put them back in my bag. David burst out laughing.

Melvin couldn't contain himself any longer.

"Give me a biscuit, you rotter," he said.

"Sell him one," said David.

I burst into laughter at the thought of selling poor Melvin a biscuit. Melvin started laughing too, he knew we were playing him up.

I looked at him and said: "You called me a rotter but you never told the char lady off, did you."

"No," Melvin agreed. "She was too far away, and at the wrong end of the train!"

David and I curled up with laughter.

We parted company at New Street and I waited in Union Street for the bus to come. There were a few different ones I could catch but I just stood there deep in thought about the day, the trip to Sheffield and Doncaster, the works and being scared stiff. When the bus arrived I went upstairs, I liked to look out of the windows as it made its way to Perry Bar. The clippy came round for the fare but I just sat there thinking about another great day out - and my supper.

I arrived home to find only Mom in.

"Hello son," she said. "Had another great day out by the look of the time."

"Oh yeah Mom, what a day to tell you about after supper time," I said.

"Do you think you've got some tea then?," she smiled

"Yes our Mom. You wouldn't let me starve now would you?," I asked.

Mom looked over at me. "You eat like a horse but never seem to put any weight on," she said.

"I do," I answered. "But all this running around these sheds and yards takes it off again."

She went on: "You should enter the races at school. Look how many prizes you would win."

"Never thought about that," I replied.

"Off to bed you go, Alex. Last week and then you're on your holidays," said Mom.

"Yes," I thought. "Liverpool and Manchester next."

The few remaining days at school were being wished away. Tuesday and Wednesday just seemed to drag by. Thursday over with and finally Friday came. Melvin wrote out the timetable for the trip to Manchester complete with the time and place to meet up, the cost of the trip plus bus fares to the different depots. Other trips were planned for the holidays too - Liverpool, Swansea, Leeds, Sheffield and Chesterfield. Melvin was especially looking forward to Swansea, it was a place he had never been to before.

HOLIDAY MONEY

The last day at school was a free day. You had to come to school but, within reason, you could do what you wanted - play games, bring in a record player and play records, play footy or just talk to your mates in other classes. It was by far the best day in the school calendar and everyone looked forward to it. Even the teachers seemed to enjoy it.

There would always be some smart Alec who would start the countdown, usually from about one minute to 4 o'clock, 60-59-58 and so on. By the time we reached 20 the whole class was in on the act. Then by the final 10 seconds everyone was larking about in total silliness. The entire school was now in final countdown to zero but, as usual, the person in charge of the bell did not ring it at zero, there was a pause and the whole school would boo him. When the noise died down came his cue to ring the bell and a great cheer went up.

The school emptied as if the plague had just arrived, teachers trying to wish everyone a wonderful holiday and remind them that the first day back was shown on the letter we took home with us.

Melvin, David and I were met by the fourth lad who sometimes came on our trips with us. He wished us all a really great holiday and left. He would not be with us on any of the trips to come. We knew that just before the Christmas holiday he had met up with a girl but we never let on that we knew. He was still a good friend and would always remain so.

Melvin and I wished David a good two weeks holiday with his parents and reminded him not to spend all his dosh on amusements.

"Remember, you'll need some for our trips out," we said.

David left to catch his bus home while Melvin and I plotted Sunday's trip to Crewe, Stafford and Wolverhampton.

I never told my mom or dad that I had saved up a few quid before the summer holidays - this was a bit sneaky but I was hoping for some extra dosh from Mom and Dad since we weren't going away this year. I would certainly need a fair bit of dosh for the trips to come, plus some for a new pad and for the film that was being developed.

I arrived home just before half-four; the key was on the string. By that I knew no-one was in because when someone was in the string was hung up behind the door. Mom was the first to arrive home from work and I had the tea all ready - all she had to do was cook it. She was always grateful for the work I did around the house, said it was a great time saver for her.

I heard my dad come in from work and take his coat off. Mom asked me to pass his dinner through the serving hatch.

"No, I'll take it to him," I said.

"I wonder why all this fuss?," said Mom.

"You know me, Mom," said I. "Always there with a helping hand."

"More like a help yourself, you mean."

It was Dad's turn to have a say. "So long as I have my tea I don't mind if the budgie brings it."

Mom and I started to laugh. We were imagining the poor old budgie flying into the living room with Dad's tea on its back. Even Dad raised a wry smile.

Mom asked: "Do you want the salt and pepper?"

"Yes, send it in with the cat," said Dad. Everyone started laughing again.

All the time this wise cracking was going on I was thinking to myself that this was the ideal way to start the holidays, everyone laughing and putting each other in the right frame of mind.

"I must time my approach to Mom and Dad for some holiday dosh. I think the best move is to ask for a lot in one... no, erm, maybe a week at a time. No, that's no good either, Mom and Dad may spend too much then that will leave them both short and this in turn will leave me short for the last couple of trips before going back to school. Oh what the hell, I'll ask for it all in one go but I'll ask a bit later on."

I was sitting quietly when Mom and Dad called me into the kitchen.

"Cor, now what," I thought to myself. "I haven't been naughty this week, nor any other week that I can think of. All the jobs are done so it's not that either."

I entered the kitchen and spotted the money on the table. Mom and Dad had been quietly going through the business of sorting out the wages, counting in my dad's holiday pay and my mom's money. We sat there going through what we would spend it on - the house, what we needed for days out....This went on for over an hour and the money was getting less and less by the minute. Finally, it was down to coppers.

"That's it," Dad declared, "all the money has been divided up into sections. This will cover the two weeks your Mom and I are off work for our holidays; that's for the few things we need for the house, there's some money for the odd day out."

My mouth was dropping lower and lower - the more the money went here and there, the more my mouth dropped.

"This little lot is for Mom and I and your Uncle Fred to go out twice down the dogs."

"The dogs," I thought, "the dogs are having more dosh than I am. This hard earned dosh is going to be spent down the dog track at Perry Bar."

Mom got up from the table. "I'll put the kettle on for a nice cuppa tea, Bill."

"Yes, a cuppa will go down a treat after all this counting."

I thought: "Forget the tea, what about my cut?" I looked towards the table. There was only about eight or nine bob left unaccounted for, plus a few pennies.

"Thanks for your help, son," my dad said.

"Okay Dad, any time you want me to sit and watch all your money disappear just give me a call."

Mom jumped in: "Don't be cheeky!"

"Only pulling Dad's leg."

"Well mind you do. Tea up!," she shouted.

Mom and Dad both just sat there, Dad smoking and slowly drinking his cuppa. Mom talked about work and the weekend plans for shopping up town. Dad asked her if she was still going with him to the dogs on Saturday night.

While they made their plans for Saturday night, I collected up the cups, took them into the kitchen, washed up, dried up and felt really fed up. I listened in, in case there was any question about what I was doing with the holidays. I listened very carefully but could here no conversation going on at all.

"Must be something going on in the living room, it's all very quiet. I don't like the sound of this," I thought.

I went back into the living room. "Another job done," I announced.

"Yeah," Dad said, "all three cups washed and clean and put away nice and tidy I bet."

Mom looked over at Dad. "Doesn't take ten minutes to wash and dry three cups up. "Alex, pass me my handbag," she said.

"I've done all the washing up, you know."

"Handbag, now," she said again.

This was a great way to start my holiday, doing jobs around the house.

"Okay Mom, only playing you up."

"I'll play your ears in a minute, now the handbag please."

I passed her the handbag.

"It's very heavy Mom. Must be all that dosh you've saved up for your holidays and days out, and the dogs and, well I can't think of anything else just now but I'm sure something will come to me," I remarked, somewhat sarcastically.

"Yes, something will come to you in a minute - a clout round the ear," warned Mom.

"Cor Mom, you do tease a lot."

Dad jumped up from the armchair. "Joan, off upstairs to get ready, meeting Fred at eight."

"Okay Billy," she answered. "Just going to sort out one or two things from my handbag."

"Can I help you?," I asked.

She looked over in my direction. "You can help me by letting me get on."

"Oh right. Any jobs for me to get on with?," I asked her.

"No son, you've done enough for one day. Why don't you go upstairs and tidy up your bedroom?"

I went upstairs but sat looking at my loco books.

It was now coming up to half-past seven. Dad would be going out soon, Mom was still diving into her handbag and I was fed up with not knowing if I would have any extra dosh for the spotting trips we had planned.

"Not the ideal way to start a holiday off by a long chalk," I thought to myself.

"Alex!" Mom called me downstairs.

"Yes Mom?," I enquired.

"Have a look in the sideboard for me, please."

"What am I looking for?," I asked.

"It's a long, thin cardboard folder with the word Kodak written on it."

I opened the sideboard door, bent down looking for this folder. "Ah, got it Mom, this it?"

"That's the one. Good lad, now pass it over to me. Must take a look at the photos the girls brought into the shop at work for me to look at."

"Anything interesting?," I asked.

"No, not really, just some photos of the girls at the works dinner and dance."

She shuffled through the collection of prints. "They have come out very well for an old Brownie 127 camera."

I just sat there twiddling my thumbs. I really wanted to have a look at these photos but didn't want to let on that I did.

"Oh dear me," my dad said. "Look at that one all covered in soot, just like a coalman, and look at the state them pair are in."

I was getting more and more fed up with my parents' silly giggling. Finally, I could take it no more. I cracked. "Let's have a look, Mom," I said.

"That's a nice one of you, Joan," my dad added.

"Yes, that was after the first few drinks too. Yeah, a real good night out, it was."

I finally reached the point where I no longer wanted to see these photos of a load of women acting the goat at the works dinner. I sat very quietly thinking about this event until I realised she never went to any such party. I decided it was my turn to play along with them.

Dad put his coat on and said: "I'm off now Joan. It's almost 7.50, must meet up with Fred at eight." He gave Mom a small kiss and said tarrarr to me.

My mom glanced in my direction. "Do you want to look at these photos?," she asked.

"Err, yes, if you want me to see them. How many are there?"

"Twelve," she replied.

"Did they all turn out then?," I asked.

She started to count them against the number written on the outside of the folder. "Yes, 12 again."

She could not keep a straight face any longer. "Here you are," she said, passing me the photos.

"Wow!," I said. They were the loco photos I had taken and all of them had turned out. I felt very pleased with myself. Not bad for my first attempt, not bad at all.

I sat and, at length, admired my first ever photograph, of Royal Scot No. 46132 The King's Regiment Liverpool at Saltley. Then I admired the rest: Black Fives 44710 and 45034 and tank engine 42075, all taken at Aston shed and the last Swindon-built steam loco, 92220 Evening Star, also at Aston; No. 7918 Rhose Wood Hall at Snow Hill, 45104 on a local passenger at Aston station, 6858 Woolston Grange at Snow Hill, 45247 with a local at Perry Bar station, 48507 with an engineering train at Aston Junction, two more "Consuls" at Saltley - 48353 and 48218 with a Type 2 diesel in the background, and 45104 with a local coming into New Street station. I savoured each and every photo like a connoisseur savouring a fine wine.

"Alex," Mom called me from the kitchen. "Want a cuppa cocoa?"

"Oh yes please, Mom." I started going through my photos for the second time.

"They are good, eh Mom?," I shouted.

"Yes son. Some nice ones for the album."

I don't have an album, I thought to myself. "Mom, I don't have an album."

"No, I know you don't but hang on, the kettle's boiling. Just give me a tick."

"Right," she said, entering the living room, a cup of cocoa in each hand. "Go and fetch the biscuits, please, Alex."

"Right Mom, how many?"

"They're on the plate."

I passed out half each, then thought no, give a couple extra to Mom. Must be nice to her, she paid for my photos and she might have something else in store for me yet.

We had not been sat down long when she said: "Right, for a start, I've paid for your photos, for seconds there's a new film in your camera, and number three, you can come with me to town tomorrow and choose your own photo album."

"It's just like Christmas," I thought. "Loads of prezzies."

"I think that's about all," she said. "These have been bought for you because, as you know, we are not going anywhere special this year so I thought you'd be pleased with them instead of holiday money."

"I'm more than pleased, Mom," I said. Making sure not to spill my cocoa, I jumped up out of the chair and gave her a great big kiss. "Thanks, our Mom. You're one in a million."

"Yes," she said. "I feel I've spent that much on all these things for this hobby."

I sat looking at my photos a third time, but also wondering whether Mom had paid for all this lot alone or whether she had gone halves with Dad. If Dad hadn't chipped in then that meant he'll be giving me some dosh, or maybe something special too. Can't wait until he gets home.

I spent the rest of the evening in my bedroom going over the plans for Crewe on Sunday and taking a look at some of the other sheds we were going to visit on other trips that Melvin was in the process of organising. I was looking forward to every trip out but must admit the trip to Crewe this Sunday did not really appeal to me. We'd be doing the Crewe sheds anyway during the trips to Manchester and Liverpool.

I heard Dad come home about 11-ish and it wasn't long before he called me down.

"All ready for Sunday?," he asked.

"Yes thanks, Dad. Just a few things to get arranged."

"Photos came out okay did they?," he asked me.

"Yeah. I'm very pleased with them and at the first attempt they all came out. Did you see Uncle Fred?," I asked him.

"Fred was there at eight as usual. He asked after us all and how you were keeping. He also said for me to give you this."

It was a £1 note.

"Cor, that's good of Fred," I said.

"Yes, but I can go one better. No, I can go five better," said Dad, dipping his hand into his back pocket and pulling out some notes - he gave me a fiver.

"That's for the trips out to wherever you're going. Just behave."

The day had really finished on a good note, a few good notes actually. "£6 in total and the other bits, plus the dosh I've saved up. I must have nearly £10," I thought. "That will surely cover all the trips during the hols." I went off to bed with my thoughts on the coming weeks.

VANDALS!

Sunday morning! Up early, made Mom and Dad some breakfast - a bit too early for them but at least they could have a lie-in - made my sandwiches, packed some pop and sweets that Mom had bought for me along with two packets of Jammie Dodgers. These were my favourite - they were Melvin's favourite as well! Come to think of it, David never refused one either.

"Better make the most of these little extras," I thought. "Once they've gone and the holiday dosh runs out, it'll be back to running errands all over the block."

I met Melvin at New Street and after checking the locos in the station, we were on the Crewe train and ready to get the locos on the first shed we would be passing at Monument Lane.

Approaching Tipton, the train veered to the right. We were being diverted. I was looking out of the carriage window when some lads playing near the railway threw a stone in my direction. I instinctively ducked, bumping my chin on the metal bar along the top of the window. The pain was immediate and I quickly put my hand up to my chin to find wetness there. I went into the toilet to inspect the damage and by the time I got there blood was running down my neck from a cut just below my chin bone.

I grabbed a handful of green paper towels and started cleaning the blood off. There was an awful lot of blood for such a small cut and it was still ouzing out of my chin when there was a knock at the toilet door. It was Melvin who suggested I see the guard. I declined.

After a while my jaw started to hurt, then my teeth and by the time we reached Wolverhampton I was feeling a lot of pain in my mouth. Melvin took over writing down the numbers for me. By Crewe, the pain all around my mouth was threatening to spoil the day.

As usual, we were off the train and straight into Crewe North shed, the locos in there taking my mind off my discomfort. The sheds done, we took a short cut to reach the works gate by 12.30 - just in time for the first party. There were more spotters outside the works than usual. We spoke to some of the lads but had no idea what was going on. Melvin went to find a commissionaire; he had not been gone for a minute when one of the lads we saw earlier came over and told me that unless I had a permit I was not going in.

Melvin returned and by the look on his face there was more bad news, and my mouth was hurting again. The dash round the sheds and all the locos had taken my mind off the pain but now it was back.

Melvin looked very angry as he stood there before us. "F.... it," he blurted out. "F.....it!"

I just stood there in total disbelief at what I was hearing. Never had I heard Melvin talk this way. During all our times together, Melvin, David or I never used bad language.

The lad that had been talking to me walked away, trying hard not to laugh. Melvin quickly calmed down.

"Sorry Alex," he said, "but someone has messed up the whole day for us."

"How's that?," I asked.

"Two weeks ago someone in the afternoon party going round the paint shop..." I knew exactly what he was going to tell me.

"What did this someone do?," he continued. "They only wrote on the side of a freshly painted engine, didn't they."

My head just dropped.

"So," Melvin continued, "there's a ban on anyone going in the paint shop, not only that but if you don't have a pass you don't get in the works."

I looked at Melvin and said: "Look, the two commissionaires know us, they know that we weren't here on that day and that we would never do anything like that. Let's wait for it to go quiet, then approach them and see what happens."

Melvin agreed. "Okay, but it's not looking good."

"Well, we can only try our hardest to get in." Some of the other lads decided to move off. We waited.

Eventually, only a handful were left standing around the works entrance. We were just about to try our approach when a commissionaire came out and told us that he was really sorry but because of what had happened there was no chance of us getting in without a permit. Some lads pleaded with him, others just walked away. Melvin and I approached him, he knew us but in a sympathetic voice said: "I'm sorry boys. Let things die down a bit. Come back in a month, I'll still be here and you'll be alright."

We thanked him and set off for Gresty Lane. I'd forgotten about my mouth but my thoughts were with another agony - how many locos I'd missed on the works. All the way to the little sub-shed Melvin never said a word.

Gresty lane done, we made our way to Crewe South. There were plenty on and, as usual, we split up to save time. Melvin was already back when I returned from my round and I could see he was still in a very bad mood.

"Must try and get him out of it or the day will just fall apart and the trip will become a real drag," I thought to myself. We still had Stafford to do and the three sheds and the small works at Wolverhampton.

I moved a few yards away from Melvin and asked him: "Did you see any locos with paint on?"

He stopped in his stride, took one look at me, then chased me all the way back to the station.

He caught up with me outside the station entrance. "It's a good job you had a few yards start on me," he spluttered, out of breath.

"Rubbish, I could have started level with you and still got to the station a week before you," I said, continuing my merciless wind-up of poor Melvin. "Come on, we'll go back and start together. Better than that, I'll give you a five-yard start and I'll still be in the station eating my Jammie Dodgers before you."

Melvin looked at me, suddenly, our race could not be further from his mind.

"How many Jammie Dodgers have you got?," he quizzed.

"Two packets, why?," I answered quietly, as if to keep this precious information from the general public around us.

"Two packets, you say."

"Yeah, two unopened packets," I said.

Melvin placed his arm around my shoulder then said: "All this running around makes me hungry."

"Yes," I agreed, "especially for JDs."

"Yes," said Melvin, "especially for two packets of JDs." We both laughed.

Crewe station on a summer Sunday afternoon was a hive of activity with trains coming thick and fast and the spotters out in force. There must have been a few hundred there, some taking photos, others telling of trips they had been on, showing their pads to others around them, swapping tales of how they bunked this shed or fiddled their way into that yard. They came from all over the country, travelling thousands of miles between them just to collect loco numbers. To everyone this hobby was a great adventure. The atmosphere was always one of great friendliness, they all seemed interested in you and you in them. There was always someone with a tale to tell, and someone else with a longer tale to tell - then we had the storyteller who could really stretch it out just to get some form of notoriety that his tale would be by far the best you had ever heard.

By now my mouth only hurt when I ate my snap, and when I tried to prize the jam and biscuit from between my teeth. These Jammie Dodgers are great but they do stick to your teeth.

Eventually, our train to Stafford was announced. Melvin and I bade our friends farewell and climbed aboard. We each occupied a window, the sort with the old leather straps. As the train eased out of the station, we pulled our windows down and waved everyone good-bye. It seems silly, but it gave you quite a lift when you saw a whole load of spotters all wave back, shouting "See you again soon."

Throughout the rest of the summer holidays we did all the trips we planned except Swansea. We did all the Manchester sheds with the help of our invaluable Shed Directory - 9E Trafford Park, 26F Patricroft, 26B

Agecroft, 26A Newton Heath, 9G Gorton shed and works, 9A Longsight and then Reddish hoping for plenty of Tommy locos, and finally 9B Stockport Edgeley and 9F Heaton Mersey. We did three sheds in Liverpool - 27A Bank Hall, 27E Walton-on-the-Hill, and 8A Edge Hill. This was a massive shed, through some arches, with engines all over the place - Coronations, Jubilees, Scots, Black Fives. We also did the Leeds sheds, starting with 55H Neville Hill, then 55B Stourton, 55A Holbeck, 56C Copley Hill and 55C Farnley Junction, followed by 55E Normanton on the way back to Sheffield. We made other trips to Yorkshire, covering all the sheds in the Bradford and Wakefield areas. We also went back to Sheffield, Canklow, and to Chesterfield to cover the Staveley sheds - 41E Barrow Hill and 41H Central, plus 41J Langwith and 18C Hasland which we had often passed on the train. It was a heavy day this one, the sheds were far apart and we spent a lot of time on buses.

Seeing the locos wasn't the only thing I enjoyed about our hobby. I also enjoyed the other things of interest we saw while travelling, such as the huge nets slung above the railway around Chesterfield to protect the trains from any coal that might fall from the buckets travelling overhead on aerial ropeways between the various collieries.

On the last Sunday before going back to school, we did the Leicester sheds, 15E Leicester Central first -another bus ride - then 15C Leicester Midland which was near the station. From there we continued to the Nottingham sheds, including Annesley and Colwick, with Derby shed and works plus Burton on the way home, and that was it - summer, 1962 over.

One of the Manchester sheds we did in the 1962 summer holidays was 26A Newton Heath. On 17th March, 1962, two Jubilees were lurking just inside the shed while Royal Scot No. 46105 *Cameron Highlander* was being prepared for its return home to Glasgow. *(Photo by Peter Wood)*

INJURY & INSULTS

As soon as the train arrived in Crewe station I was across the footbridge and into the North shed, then quickly through the fence and up towards the works gate - my full intention on this solo trip being to bunk into the works with a party.

As usual there were plenty of lads waiting for the official 12.30 party. Those who had come from far away were holding on to their permits like they were gold bars. Those who lived local also had permits. Then there was my crowd of hopefuls.

This wasn't to be my day. I didn't get in and, like some others, hung around for a while.

If you went a short distance away from the main gate you could catch the party walking under a small road bridge and I had, on past occasions, dropped in behind them. The lads knew the tricks and would smuggle you into the group. Most were great but on this day it was not to work.

I dropped behind the party and thought to myself: "I'm in." But one chap opened his mouth. The party came to a stand and the commissionaire told me to clamber back the way I had fallen in. I said sorry but to no avail, Alex was out and that was that.

I followed the road which led to another works entrance further along from the main gates, one where the workers entered via a footbridge. On the other side was a hut where two old lads worked as watchmen. Eventually, I reached a spot close to a very high corrugated fence where you could climb a little way up some steps and just see a couple of locos outside the main workshops.

There were already too many spotters on the steps and because I was small and thin I was pushed out by some of the bigger boys. Still, I was determined to get these locos and no mistake about it.

A small but very thick log was leaning against the corrugated iron fence, offering me a step up so that I could see over the top and get the locos inside.

Pad in my left hand, pen in my right, I climbed very carefully up. The top of the fence was very sharp and pointed but I was able to stand there nice and quiet and before long I had managed to write down eight numbers.

I was just about to get down when this big kid decided to join me on the log. It wasn't wide enough for two of us. He put his big left boot on the log and just as he pushed himself up from the ground his force was so much that he pushed me off and I fell to my left. I instinctively lifted my left hand to save myself by grabbing the top of the fence. Immediately, the sharp metal ripped into my pad and fingers. The shock made me cry out. I pulled my hand away and fell to the floor, my pad by my side. The big kid also fell.

The blood from the cuts between my three fingers was really pumping out and I was crying from the shock and the pain. The other kid got up off the floor, said sorry then called some of the others over to help. They started calling to the old lads in the hut. At first they only looked over at all these lads shouting - must have thought they were just larking about. Time was passing and the sight of all this blood was making me feel sick. Again they tried to summon help and eventually one chap, on seeing the blood, came over and then hurried to open the gates. He ushered me into the hut and took a look at the cuts.

The other old chap called me everything, a barrage of Fs, Bs and one or two less mentionable words. This was no time for anger, I was in a lot of pain with blood still pouring from the deep cuts to my fingers. A phone call was made and a chap came to give me first aid.

He came into the hut just as the old chap was well into his second salvo of abuse. I don't know what hurt the most, the pain or this bloke turning on me the way he did. The young first aider who had been called from the main works took a long look at the mess my hand was in. Then, without hesitation, he hurried me into the works and a small first aid room. I was trying my best to remember the numbers I saw on the way.

As I stood there with this first aider bathing my fingers I began to feel really scared at what damage the corrugated fence might have done to my fingers. He was shaking his head as he bathed them. I began to imagine the worst - I might loose them.

Another first aider popped his head round the office door, In his hands were two cups of tea and a couple of biscuits laid out neatly on a small plate. He then closed the door behind him. I said thankyou but I don't think he heard me. The chap that was fixing up my hand was by now tutting to himself as he gently wrapped a bandage over and between my fingers.

The chap who had brought the tea glared at me for a second or two, tidied up the mess and then glanced at me again as I stood there motionless. Then he said, half smiling: "I've heard of many ways to get locos but never knew of anyone going this far."

I tried to laugh but the throbbing from my hand prevented me from appreciating his joke. Then he asked me for the truth behind the accident, he had to make an entry in the accident book. I explained all that had happened to me except that part about being slung out while trying to bunk in from the road bridge - I didn't feel this had any bearing on the accident.

He wrote down everything I said word for word then closed the book and escorted me back towards the hut. A few yards short of the hut he got hold of my right arm. "Stop a minute," he said.

I stopped on a sixpence. He walked over into the hut and the old chap who helped came out and asked if I was okay.

"Yes thankyou," I said. "And thanks for calling the first aid chap for me."

He then advised me to move a few more yards away from the hut. From what I could make out, the first aid chappy was really going to town on the other poor old lad. I could just make out the odd swear word. Then the hut door opened and out walked the first aider. He looked really mean. "And that's in my .....ing report as well," he said. The three of us stood for a moment, laughing to ourselves.

"Right," said the first aider in turning to the more pleasant old lad, "You take this young lad to the main entrance and make sure you go via all the works - and don't miss the paint shop.

The first aid chap held out his hand to shake mine and as we shook hands I asked: "How bad is it?"

"Oh, more blood than damage. You should be okay in a week or two, but don't use it. Tell your mom and dad to take you down to the local doctor's for him to look at it and change the dressing, okay son?"

"Yes, yes, and thanks for your help mister."

He turned and I watched him walk back into the workshops.

The old lad and I continued our trip round but he had to write down all the loco numbers for me. I think he enjoyed it as every now and then a smile came across his face. He was clever in his final move. We had caught up with the party which was a few yards in front of us. He said that as they had almost reached the main gate we would join them at the last second. He didn't want anyone to see me being shepherded separately from the party as this might cause someone to start asking awkward questions.

At the final moment he said: "Tarrar son" then mingled me into the tail end of the party. I mingled in the best I could, I wanted to turn and wave goodbye but this would not have been the right move to make. I left the works entrance feeling really bad inside and my thoughts were on getting myself straight back home.

Once back at the station I got on the first Birmingham train, the day was over for me but the bad news wasn't. First, I'd forgotten to ask the old lad for the numbers he had written down for me and, second, I could not hold my pad to write down any numbers I saw on the way home.

As the week passed, the hand gradually improved. The doctor told me that if I had fallen straight down my fingers would have been so badly damaged that they would have had to be amputated, that's if the fence had not cut them straight off.

CUT SHORT

Winter was starting early this year and the forecasts were not good at all. The talk was of a very bad winter in store for the whole country, possibly the worst since 1947.

During the early autumn we concentrated on local trips - giving ourselves chance to build up the dosh we needed for longer trips to come. By the dark days of late November, we had managed to get to such places as March, Peterborough, Worcester, Gloucester, Bristol and Bath.

The trip to March and Peterborough had been better than we expected. With Leicester on the way home, we saw a grand total of 326 locos and I copped just over half of them, even better than the trip to Doncaster.

In Bath we followed Melvin to the Somerset and Dorest Railway shed at Green Park - a nice shed with about 20 locos on. It wasn't far from the station which seemed to be set in such a peaceful and picturesque area. It was a pity we never had time to appreciate the architectural beauty of places like this but our hobby was too fast for that. Melvin regularly told us the time to keep us on the move, no matter where we were. We had to keep up the speed of the trip and not run late for any of our train connections.

On this particular trip we saw a total of 238 locos and I copped 89. Out of 43 locos on Bristol Bath Road shed only one was steam, No. 6972 Beningbrough Hall. There was a good variety of diesels though.

On the way back our train came to a stand at the foot of the famous Lickey Incline, the fearsome 1 in 37 climb up to Barnt Green and Birmingham. Here, five Pannier tank locos waited, coupled together, ready to help any heavy train up the bank, whether a humble goods or a proud express passenger - they all needed the help of these powerful little tanks.

We waited patiently for the tank locos to come up behind us and start pushing. The shrill of the locos' whistling was a sound to be heard, our steam engine whistled and then, with the five tanks opening up behind us and with the different motions going, it was a sight to be savoured. White and black smoke errupted from the line of chimneys all the way up. At the top, they stopped, waited a little while, whistled goodbye, then slowly disappeared back down the bank as we pulled away out of their sight.

Melvin had already worked out our next trip but he never announced it until we were back at school on Monday morning, so we eagerly awaited his arrival in the playground. This time, bright and cheerful, he announced that we would be off to Guildford and Feltham via Reading. These were new places for me and he asked me to bring my camera - great stuff!

Early start on Sunday, 25th November, 1962, bag all packed on Saturday - pad, pens, ruler, camera, directory and plenty of snap and pop, not forgetting a couple of packets of Jammie Dodgers. No trip would seem right with-

59

out them.

By the time we reached Reading we had collected over 60 locos just from the sheds we passed on the way - Tyseley, Leamington, Banbury, Oxford, Didcot and the main shed at Reading. We did the small sub shed at Reading then were on our way to Guildford. This was another good shed but just as I was taking some photos it started snowing. The bus journey to Feltham seemed to take forever, then we had to get another bus to get on to the shed. By this time the snow was falling very heavily and when we finally got there it was very bad under foot.

We were in and out of Feltham very fast, there was no time to hang about - the weather was getting worse by the minute. We boarded our first bus out, then onto another bus to Southall station and the shed, 81C. We had passed the shed before on our trips to London, but we were in for a pleasant surprise - it was a lot bigger than it looked from the main line and was full with 49 on. This over and done, we headed off for the train to Didcot, 81E - and a chance for some snap and to get warmed up.

At Didcot the weather was very very bad indeed so we decided that it should be done another time and stayed put on the train until Oxford. Here we jumped off, ran round the shed and caught the next train home.

This was the first time that we had cut short a trip but we did not want to get stuck in the bad weather. Also, we had no idea what the weather might be like nearer home - it could be even worse.

We were still wet and cold from our journey between Guildford and Feltham and it took us a long time to warm up. This was a bad day to be out. We kept our spirits up by talking about the new sheds we'd bunked and how many locos we thought we had copped. We tried very hard to take an interest in the sheds that were to come on the way home but we only peered through the glass instead of opening the windows as we would normally do. The good old Jammie Dodgers came to the rescue, some extra for the lads - just a 'pick-me-up' at the right time. Before long we were emerging from the tunnel into Snow Hill station and we were safely home.

The three of us were very suprised when we got out into the cold night air to find the snow worse here than at any of the places we had been. The city had caught the full force of what would be the worst weather for 15 years. I was very glad to get home for a good hot supper and my folks were glad to see me back safely. They had been worried about me ever since the snow started to fall just after dinner time.

I had a nice warm by the fire, a hot wash then into bed. My eyes closed as my head hit the old feather pillow and I was gone for the night.

TROUBLE IN SCHOOL

Monday morning, another day at school to get through. I really felt bad this day and the thought of spending all day in a classroom never really appealed to me but when you'd had your pleasure, you had to put up with the pain, and going to school could get no more painful than it would be today.

Mom had called me a few times but my scrawny little body was fighting it all the way to the carpet.

"You'll be late for school, Alex!," she shouted.

"Okay Mom, getting up now."

Not really. I was still lying there, not having moved a muscle. But I had to make the effort. I didn't want to be late and start the week off badly.

Eventually I managed to drag myself downstairs to the kitchen. Mom examined me closely, pushing my head from one side to the other as she peered into my eyes and felt my forehead.

"You don't look very well to me," she said.

"I'm just a bit tired from the trip yesterday - feel a bit rough because of the bad weather we got caught up in," I explained.

"Well, the snow's still out there, so is school. Your dad's gone off early so as not to be late for work. I'm off soon so get your skates on."

"Yes Mom, not to worry. I'll get there. Don't worry about me feeling poorly. I'll struggle on to the end of the road," I moaned.

"If you have a day off school don't expect to go number collecting at the weekend," said Mom firmly.

"It's okay Mom, I feel a bit better now," I replied.

"I bet you do," Mom said. "It's amazing how a few seconds can make a difference."

She took a quick, sharp look in my direction. "Feeling better has nothing to do with the weekend trainspotting has it Alex?"

"No no Mom - must be that nice warm cup of tea you gave me, and the extra toast. My tummy feels as though it's on fire"

"Well get a move on or you'll feel your bum on fire after my hand slaps it." In the old days down Aston my mom was a lady not to be messed with and she would give you a clout if need be, but she'd also give you her last penny.

I kept up the act until reaching the downstairs landing that led from our maisonnette to the ground floor.

Outside it was another world - not a dog in sight, traffic held up, people scurrying about their business, kids all wrapped up. Everything was a mucky white - there was slush in the gutters, on the pavement and vehicles were filthy dirty. All this and it was only Monday morning! I still had the rest of the week to go yet. Things had to get better by Sunday - the thought of staying indoors at the weekend was a real drag. It's bad enough having to go to school but no trip out, that's not funny at all.

The closer to school I got, the more snowball raids I became involved in. Well, you had to throw some back at those who were throwing them at you or you would be bombarded by the rest of the raiders. It was great fun, snowballs coming at you from every direction. You hit someone and they would aim at you. Then others would gang up on you and you were in for a real tough time trying to dodge every snowball that headed in your direction. There was no way out of it - you either fired back or you got bombed.

The playground was a battle zone. Everyone was bombing each other. Some who were a little on the daring side would propel one in the direction of a teacher coming into the playground, then watch as it slowly headed towards the teacher's feet. You never aimed higher than that because you could hurt someone, namely the teacher and that would not be a good way to start the week.

I didn't see Melvin or David until we were in class. I must say, they looked as lousy as I felt but we were in for the day so we just had to make the best of it.

The bell for break was a welcome sound. The monitors had already brought in the crates of milk and everyone got a bottle. Those who didn't want it gave it to a friend. The same happened with dinners. Some of the boys who didn't feel like dinner gave their ticket to someone else. My Mom, without fail, always gave me half a crown dinner money on Monday morning and when I got home she always asked to see my remaining four tickets. Some lads flogged their dinner tickets for money. The ticket was sixpence for every school day, five each week. Every week's was a different colour so you couldn't keep one from last week and expect a dinner with it this week.

Talking of school dinners, the dinner ladies were the most important people in the school, even ranking above your own friends and the teachers. By helping them carry a heavy tray or something back from the hall to the kitchens you could improve your chances of getting seconds no end.

The dinner bell was rung by one of the more trusted boys. For those who stayed dinners this was, apart from the 4 o'clock bell, the best part of the day. We were all seated in the very large school hall and the cooks brought the food round on trolleys. There were so many of us that by the time they got to the last ones with their first courses, the first ones were on their puddings.

The dinners were a double scoopof mash, peas and carrots, mincement, gravy, or some days it was sausage and chips. Pudding was a large dish of apple tart and custard. I licked my lips at the thought of it. Other days it was treacle sponge and custard, rice pudding, sago or jam rolly poly and custard, with seconds if you were lucky - or well in with the dinner ladies.

Some lads took their time on purpose so they could help push the heavy trolleys back to the kitchens, others helped put the large food trays away. I have even known boys rush their dinner down, including seconds, and then hurry to the kitchen so they could help with the washing up, quite prepared to miss out on a game of footy in the playground. All in the name of staking their claim to seconds.

There were some kids in our school from poor families - and the dinner ladies always gave them extra grub and they would be first up for seconds if any were going. I've also known some lads give one of their sandwiches, or a dinner ticket to lads who had very little - just so they got something to eat. Even in that hard winter of 1962 many a lad had cardboard shoes and holes in his socks. Some were so poorly dressed you could not understand how they got this far in life. It hurt to look at them.

The teachers were fully aware of the situation but were powerless to do much about it, though they did help whenever they could. Everyone had the same opportunities in class, those who were a little on the slow side were give every chance to keep level with the rest.

The class I remained in from Day One at Birchfield Road Secondary Modern was in the A stream and quite a mixture there was of us. I started the same day with a lad from Italy. There were also some Irish kids, an Indian and some West Indians but all these years later most of their names escape me.

During the course of the day Melvin had not mentioned anything about the weekend. He finally came over in the afternoon break to say that he had not felt good and wanted to keep himself to himself. We were in the same boat so we knew how he was feeling.

"I will have a look at a plan sometime towards the weekend because the weather could be our guideline. A trip to London looks possible weather-wise," he said.

The thought of another trip to London right now did not excite me like the trips we had made there before.

I arrived home just after ten-past four. A fter changing quickly into some warm clothes, I grabbed a brush and shovel and went straight out looking for snow to clear for the neighbours - to show them what a good lad I was, oh and to try and earn some dosh for the next trip out.

This London trip was back on my mind. Somehow it was not a trip I want-ed to go on but I would have to wait and see what the weather was like. Maybe Melvin was right, he rarely made an error of judgement on our trips.

A few paths done and a few quid in my pocket already. A feel a lot better. A few more to do before the folks get home and I get the tea ready.

During the rest of the week the snow was still well in evidence across the whole country. Birmingham, the North, South, East and West were all having it bad. What could be worse is that we do not go out on a trip anywhere - that would be worse than London.

Come Friday we waited for Melvin in the front playground. I hoped we would be off to some new sheds but it was not to be. Melvin confirmed that we were going to London because the weather was not as bad there as other places.

I awoke early on saturday morning, looked out of the window and saw only the same sight that I had seen all week - snow and a grey sky. This was it, I thought, until our London trip tomorrow. After breakfast I sat and counted up the money left from last weekend, money I had earned from running errands and the extra dosh from snow clearing.

Looking forward as always, Melvin took a piece of paper from his pocket. "It's about time we went down to Eastleigh, we can do another Southern shed on the way - Basingstoke," he announced.

I chipped in: "There's a massive works at Eastleigh isn't there Melv?"

"I know," he answered. "Its bigger than you think and I know the way in."

"Cor, sounds like a good one," said David.

"Yes," said Melvin again. "And we can do Oxford and Banbury on the way home. It might just make up for yesterday - did you cop many Alex?"

"Not really, 57."

"How about you David?," Melvin asked.

"Just over 40-odd," David answered.

"The second trip is to another new place at Oswestry via Shrewsbury," continued Melvin.

I looked at both David and Melvin, never been there, never even heard of them. I asked Melvin if he had ever been there before.

"No," came his reply. "That's why I thought we would go. It's a new shed for all of us. The trip is only local so we won't spend much dosh before the Christmas hols. We do Cardiff as soon as the holidays are over and then get to Swansea sometime."

After assembly, Mr. Davies did the register. It was a common thing on a Monday for some lads to be missing, they were at home looking after their brothers or sisters while their moms and dads were out at work, or they were poorly. All sorts of letters would arrive the next day. You could tell by the teacher's reaction when a letter gave a really good excuse.

Mr. Davies would smile to himself, then shake his head slowly, look up at the class over his half-moon glasses and very politely ask the lad who had brought the letter how long he had taken to think this one up. The lad would in all seriousness claim it to be a true account of why he was off school.

Of course, that was the cue for the rest of the class to burst into laughter.

Mr. Davies let us have our moment of fun and then called the class to order.

Today was not to be much fun for me though. We had an African teacher called Mr. Obungwanna - I think that's how it was spelt. During the rush to the playground for break, one of the boys walking behind him called out a name that sounded like his but was something quite different. He turned to see who had said it and I was the first boy he saw. He thought it was me, reported me and I received three of the best from Mr. Smith.

I took the punishment without a word but after class I informed Mr. Obungwanna that I never called his name and that I would never be so disrespectful. I then told Mr Smith the same. Finally, I headed off to see the headmaster, Mr. J. Holdham. It was said he played for Warwickshire Cricket Club and I was a member of our winning school cricket team in the 1961/2 seasons, a useful connection, I thought. He said he would speak again with me on a later date which I felt was a fair response.

The next afternoon I was informed by Mr. Davies that I must report to the headmaster immediately. This I did, knocking on his door. His secretary opened it and asked me to wait as Mr. Holdham was busy. I sat on one of four chairs outside his office and waited patiently. Another boy came out with his mom; he was crying for some reason. I was then summoned into Mr. Holdham's office. Standing there with my arms behind my back, I waited for him to speak. He put a diary away into a desk, sat down and looked up at me.

"Good afternoon, Mr. Holdham, you wanted to see me," I said.

"Yes, Scott," he answered, "just wait a while, I'm expecting the two masters who have been involved in this unfortunate incident."

The word unfortunate could have a double meaning, I thought to myself. Was it an unfortunate mistake, or would it be unfortunate for me?

Mr. Obungwanna was first to knock and be asked to enter. He was followed by Mr. Smith but another knock followed and in came Mr. Davies which seemed to suprise the headmaster.

Mr. Holdham asked me to leave his office, saying he would call me in due course. I eased my way past the three masters who had since been joined by Mr. Holdham's secretary.

Again, I sat outside and waited, wondering if I was in big trouble and what would happen to me. This was a situation which could bring me all sorts of difficulties. Mr. Obungwanna was new to the school and I thought that this could turn out really bad for me. I was getting really upset.

The door opened and Mr. Obungwanna came out. He glanced at me then tilted his head forward. Mr. Smith was next out, he came close to me and said he would speak to me in private later that afternoon. Last out was my teacher, Mr. Davies. He walked over to me, ruffled my hair, smiled and said: "See you in class."

The door opened again and Mr. Holdham's secretary called me in. Mr. Holdham looked up at me and then got to his feet. He held out his right hand for me to shake. My hand slowly reached out in his direction as tears started to run down my face. I shook his hand firmly, his secretary offered me a tissue. I was crying with relief that I was not in trouble and that my mom and dad would not be getting a letter to say I'd had the cane.

Mr. Holdham's secretary comforted me by putting her arms round my shoulders. Mr. Holdham could see that I was very hurt by this experience and unable to return to my class so he let me sit outside his office for the rest of the afternoon. Just before the bell rang, he came out and told me it was home time so I left for the staff room and my private meeting with Mr. Smith. He arrived and said I should speak to Mr. Davies tomorrow.

Going out into the playground, I was surrounded by boys from our class wanting to know what had happened in the head's office. I could only tell them that I was to be spoken to again tomorrow and that I had to see Mr. Davies first thing after assembly.

Melvin and David walked so far home with me. I knew I could tell them what had happened and I knew it would go no further. They felt I had been given the cane for something I didn't do, and that it was a case of mistaken identity, but it was a bit late to argue the point as I had already had it.

I told them that when Mr. Smith gave me the cane it wasn't really that bad - he did seem to pull back with it.

All the way home, all evening and on the way back to school the next morning, my thoughts were on what was going to happen to me today, what Mr. Davies was going to say and if I was in any trouble. My stomach was churning as we went into our classroom and the moment of my one to one with Mr. Davies drew closer.

After register, Mr. Davies called me to him at the front of the class; he then walked me to the school hall. His first words were that I was not in any trouble of any kind. My heart dropped and my mouth must have opened a foot wide but inside I felt so much relief that I didn't know what to do. Mr. Davies went on to explain that another boy had been in to explain that he knew it was not me who had made the remark about Mr. Obungwanna - but neither did he know who had.

WAGGERS

The third Sunday morning on the trot we all met up at Snow Hill, at our usual time of 9.30. Tickets in our hands ready for the nice lady to clip, we made our way down to the platform where, as per our usual routine, we walked round noting any locos that were in the station.

A porter placed the indicator board facing the line on which our train to Paddington was due. At 9.55 it was announced and we looked down towards the platform end, eagerly waiting to see which loco would be pulling us. It was a Grange last time so what would it be today? A King maybe.

We kept looking but there was nothing to see, no smoke or steam beyond the bridge and it was now four minutes to ten. Suddenly, there it was - a diesel. We just stood with our mouths open at this apparition grinding its way slowly towards us. I looked at David, he was trans-fixed. Melvin was shaking his head from side to side in disbelief.

The fact was that it was clean, it looked proud of itself, it was there and you could feel it wanted to talk to you. I'm sure it wanted to say: "Here I am, I'm ready to go, so let's go. I'll get you there, honest I will."

We scrambled into a compartment and shut the door. There was a loud hoot, a sudden jerk, a whistle was blown and with a mighty roar from the engines, we moved off.

We just sat together in the compartment, no-one spoke. We never dimmed the light to play ghosts in the darkness of the tunnel - though we often played the goat! Melvin was, I'm sure, thinking of that day at Rugby when all those Patriots had their chimneys covered with rags. Were our much cherished Kings also now in store somewhere?

As we passed Tyseley shed, Melvin asked out loud: "Why is there no King pulling us?"

David sat quietly looking at his Locoshed book to see if he had copped anything so far.

I thought about the photos I had taken just the week before - Duchess class Pacific No. 46250 City of Lichfield at New Street and, at Snow Hill, Grange No. 6811 Cranbourne Grange. I was just looking in my shedbook to see if I had copped it when a diesel, No. D1000, entered the station from the London direction. It was a sandy colour and the nameplate on its side said Western Enterprise.

Then I remembered our trip to Guildford and Southall. On the way out we saw two of these locos double-headed - D1000 again and D1001. I drew Melvin's attention to this and we tried hard to think where we saw them. I thought they were in the carriage sidings at Tyseley.

Gradually, we got over the shock of this new phenomenon and began discussing our plans for the day.

"Okay lads, this the plan." Melvin pointed out that on entering Reading station we had to hurry off the train.

"It stops near the subway. Next we must travel from Reading to Eastleigh through Basingstoke. There's a good little shed there but we will do it on the way back."

I raised my hand to ask a question - Melvin and David started laughing at me.

"We're not in school now," they said together.

I joined in - laughter was always a highly infectious thing in our little group. "Sorry, I forgot."

Then we stopped laughing and got down to the serious business of taking down the numbers on Leamington shed. The shed passed, it was back to the plan.

Without thinking, I half raised my arm again.

"Yes Alex, what is it?" asked Melvin.

"Is there any reason why we are doing Basingstoke after Eastleigh?"

"We must do the works first because the party goes round at between two and two thirty," explained Melvin. "We have no permit so we must beat them by getting in then, getting round and getting out quickly."

The Western loco at the front all forgotten, Melvin told us about the size of the works at Eastleigh, and the shed. He made a point of telling us about the third rail and how dangerous it was. We were at full attention to his every word on Eastleigh. I asked him about the train from Reading to Eastleigh.

"Oh yes," said Melvin. "It's a unit, usually in the bay platform so if we hurry we can be on the.." He stopped and rolled back his shirt sleeve to look at his watch. "Errmm, right let's see. We should, if everything runs smoothly, catch the 12.23."

At Reading we dived off the train and ran as fast as our legs could carry us. Melvin was a big lad but he could get a sprint on when need be and we just managed to get on board as the train was being signalled out. We slammed the door and were on our way. My heart was pounding like a machine gun.

After stopping at every station en-route, the train rolled into Eastleigh station. Out of the station we started running again, following Melvin. We ran for a good few hundred yards, then up a slope which took us over the railway lines. Half-way over the bridge, Melvin called us to a halt.

"Walk slowly," he said. "Just look over the bridge in the opposite direction to the lads that are standing outside the works entrance. Take it real steady."

We were over the bridge. I never once looked at those who were waiting but just looked towards where we were going. We passed the shed entrance on our right, then Melvin told us to run and follow him. We ran for another few hundred yards and this time we were at the back of the works.

Thoughts of Doncaster came to my mind. We found a small gap in the fence and slipped our bags through to Melvin who was first in. David was next, then me.

"Keep together and just stick to the plans we have made," said Melvin.

Once inside we kept very close together. We could hear voices so there were some people still working on the locos - we did not wish to disturb them.

We got every number of every loco in the works and were back at the shed entrance before the official party had even left to go round. The only locos we missed were those at the front entrance.

The shed next, we split up, each taking the area Melvin had allotted us. He again reminded us of the third rail. We were on our toes for this shed, locos were everywhere. Today it was really packed out, there must have been a hundred or so on. As we left the shed, we noticed the works party had gone in but we were hurrying to the station for the next train back to Basingstoke.

Basingstoke shed done, we were at the front of the unit and on our way back to Reading where we changed for Oxford and Banbury.

We were all very pleased at getting into Eastleigh shed and works. Once again, Melvin had planned the trip perfectly. I counted up the locos that were in the works, a grand total of 56, plus those at the front that we could not get. We missed nothing on the shed and wrote down a total of 151. This must have been the most locos I had ever seen on any shed. I decided to check after school tomorrow, there had been a lot on Doncaster, and March had to be considered as there were two sheds.

"Oxford next lads, get your gear ready, we're going to bunk the shed," Melvin announced.

No-one spoke, we just slowly gathered up our books, pens, pads and put our gloves and coats on. The train slowed down and ran gently into the platform. Melvin had his head out of the window. "It's a bitter cold night lads," he said, half smiling to himself. "Stacks of people on the platform."

Snow was falling with flakes as big as half crowns. The train had almost stopped when Melvin cried out: "I think," he paused for a second. "Yes, I'm sure there are two waggers. I can see two waggers," he said excitedly.

We eventually came to a stand at the shed end of the platform. Melvin opened the door, stepped outside then hurried towards the waggers and started talking to them. The two lads came rushing towards us. "We'll watch your gear," one of the lads said. "Hurry up, hurry up."

"Come on Alex, come on David, hurry boys, get a move on!," Melvin screamed at us. David and I caught up with him.

"Listen," he said, "don't write any numbers down, just look at them, then hurry back to the train."

The three of us ran around the shed just looking at every single loco and within a few minutes we were running our guts out trying to get back to the train. The two waggers bought us time by opening carriage doors which the poor old porter had just closed. No sooner had he closed them and was on his way back up the platform than another couple would be opened by unseen hands and he'd have to trudge back yet again.

The trick worked a treat and we just made it back. The doors all closed this time, there was a whistle from the platform, another from the engine and we were pulling gently away from Oxford.

How we never sprained, broke or dislocated anything while running in semi-darkness over the ballast and track I'll never know. I suppose we were just lucky.

Once back in our warm compartment one of the other two lads called out the numbers - they had bunked the shed just before we got there.

As we approached Banbury all five of us headed to the back of the train and as soon as it came to a halt we were off and running down the track towards the shed. Once inside, Melvin quietly called off all the numbers. We wrote them down, then we all made our way back to the station to patiently await the train home to Birmingham.

We parted company with our new found friends at Snow Hill. I never saw them again but they always came into conversation whenever Melvin, David and me were out on a trip passing Banbury and Oxford.

The bus approached Perry Bar. I was off, said goodnight to the clippy and made my way over the peck, up the stairs and safely home to our front foor.

Mom answered the door, as always with a smile on her face. Dad was out down the local, probably with Uncle Fred.

"Okay Mom?," I asked her.

"Yes son," she replied, "and you?"

"Oh yeah. We had a great day out. You should see my pad. I must have seen over 400 engines." The actual number was 390 of which I copped 186, the most ever in a single trip.

She got my supper out of the oven and it looked smashing - beef, mash, pees, carrots and really thick, dark brown gravy that had stuck to the side of the plate. I lapped it up, then set about scraping the gravy from round the edge. After that it was a quick lick of the plate and a nice hot cup of cocoa to round off the day.

THE VISITOR

I didn't hear my folks come back from their night down the pub on Christmas Eve. In fact, I only woke up once and looked out of my bedroom window into the dark. The snow was still shining in the silvery moonlight from many a rooftop and glistening icicles were still hanging from black gutters and fallpipes. I had no idea of the time, I couldn't see my watch without getting out of bed and putting the light on but everything looked just the same as yesterday, and the day before that, and the week before that. No sign of this winter loosening its grip.

The next time I awoke it was daylight. I looked out of my window again. This time the scene was dull and very cold looking, just the odd kid out playing on the new bike Father Christmas had brought him.

It was almost 8.30 so I called my sister, then called again thinking she was fast asleep - still no answer. I tapped on her door, then she shouted from downstairs: "Alex, come and see all these presents!"

I didn't bother getting dressed or even washed, at least for the morning.

We decided to make Mom and Dad breakfast in bed - a treat to start the day off right. I made the tea and toast, Sheila got the double tray ready and put a few flowers in an old vase. Cereal in the dishes, two well boiled eggs and we set off upstairs with our treat. I carried the trays while Sheila knocked on the door.

"Come in," Mom said. We entered and wished them both a very merry Christmas then passed a tray to each of them.

"Oh that's nice of you Sheila," said Mom.

"Thanks son," Dad said to me.

"We both did it," Sheila told them, "but the idea was mine."

"No, it was mine," I contested.

We both started to laugh - it didn't matter whose idea it was so long as we did it.

We went back downstairs to get our own breakfast on the go - a bowl of hot porridge each, a couple of rounds of toast, a nice cup of tea, then the fire on to get the living room warmed up. The folks were eating their breakfast but it was just a matter of time before they would be washed and down for the opening of the cards first. Then Mom would start off the present opening. This was the way we always did it - Mom first, then Dad, then Sheila who always went for the biggest parcel first, and finally me.

It was just after nine o'clock, the living room was nice and cosy, the cards were all ready for opening, and we could hear Mom and Dad getting ready to come down. We sat by the presents waiting for Mom to come in and start the proceedings.

The door opened and in she walked, followed closely by Dad. Sheila shot upstairs for the breakfast crocks. I ran the hot water for the washing up and made a fresh cup of tea for Mom and Dad. Then, coming up to half nine, we were at last ready for the best part of the day.

Dad passed Mom the first present. She weighed it up, shook it for a little while, then smelt it. This was all in fun, just hanging it out so it would take longer to get to our presents. Eventually she removed the Christmas wrapping paper to reveal a black handbag, arced in shape with plenty of zip pockets for all those little things that Mom carried about with her.

"Oh thankyou, Billy," she said.

Sheila and I never spoke a word. Billy turned to Joan and told her it was us who had bought it for her and that we hoped it was the one she had been on about for the last couple of months.

"Oh yes, that's the one," she said. "That's the one I've seen in town."

"Phew, glad she liked that," I thought to myself. "Good start to the day."

Mom was full of praise for my sister and me. Dad next - he just picked up the parcels at random. The first produced a nice white shirt.

"Oh thanks Sheila, thanks Alex," he said.

"No, Mom bought you that," I said.

"Of course she did, only pulling your legs."

Mom sat there. "Oh," she said. "That's the last one I buy you."

Dad winked over at us sitting on the floor trying not to laugh because Mom was acting as though she was in a huff with Dad.

Sheila next - some underclothes.

Now my turn - all the different regional loco books. I was very pleased with the first of the day.

Now Mom again. Another time-wasting excercise in trying to guess what it is - a bottle of gin from Uncle Fred.

"That will go down a treat," she said. "Come on Bill, you're up next."

Dad moved his hand over a pile of presents still waiting to be unwrapped. "This one," he said, opening the fancy paper which revealed a hundred Park Drive. "Cor, that's one from Joan," he said.

"Smoke them outside," she joked Mom with a big grin on her face.

"Sheila again," said Dad looking at the writing on the paper -a new pair of shoes.

Sheila put them on straight away and did a short walk round the room while everyone paid the fullest attention.

"They look great," Dad said.

"Okay babe?," Mom asked her.

Oh yes, just the right size," Sheila answered.

"Alex, one for you," said Mom passing me a soft parcel. It was a new pair of footy socks - Villa. "They'll keep your legs warm when you're out on your trips."

The present opening went on for an hour or so. At about 11 o'clock, Mom stopped the day's entertainment and went into the kitchen with Dad to put the turkey in the oven. It was a very big one and kept us going for days. Besides Christmas dinner we had it for teatime sandwiches and on Boxing Day Fred and Dad took a sandwich with them down the ale house.

When Mom and Dad returned from the kitchen, Sheila and me made a cup of tea while Mom tidied up and Dad rearranged some more presents for us to open. They were scattered all over the floor - there seemed to be more then when we started.

"Off we go," said Dad. "Joan, here you are." He passed her another fair sized one.

Mom opened it at her usual slow pace, just to spin it out.

"Hurry up," quipped Dad. "It'll soon be next Christmas. Sheila and I burst out laughing but Mom took no notice, in fact she took even longer about it.

"Awe come on, Mom," I said.

"Okay," she replied. "Now let me see, which end should I open first."

We sat there shaking our heads.

Eventually the present was finally opened and guess what - a hundred Senior Service.

"All that just for some fags," I said.

We were just about to the halfway stage when Mom broke off again to get on with more dinner arrangements. Dad helped out of course while we sat and looked at the presents we had received so far. I was very pleased with the books and clothes, Sheila was still sitting around in her new shoes.

"What time will dinner be ready?," I asked Mom.

"What time is it now?," she asked me.

"It's gone past one o'clock," I shouted back to her.

"Ermm, let me see." I could hear her mumbling some words. "Say about four, no, yes say around four."

Time to get back to the order of the day. Mom started off with some stockings and a face compact. Dad with some socks and handkerchiefs. Sheila doing well with some slippers and a new dress, plus a school satchel, pens and a pencil set. My turn, two new jumpers - real flashy at that - nice and colourful. Mom off again with a headscarf and a new pinny, Dad a bottle of whisky from Fred, Sheila more school socks and a new cardy, me a pair of light brown shoes - the new sort, without carboard soles - a couple of vests, some ankle socks for the summer. By just after three it was all over except we always kept one last present back for after dinner. Mom always kept these very well hidden.

At quarter to four Mom asked Sheila to help Dad and me lay the table as dinner would be ready in about twenty minutes, also to set out the crackers. The table looked great - now for the scoff.

73

The room was getting very stuffy by now - Mom and Dad both smoked and a grey haze had replaced most of the air. With only a few minutes to go, I went out onto the balcony for a gulp of fresh air. I left the door slightly open to let some of the smoke out and then looked over the railings to see what was going on in the rest of the world around our maisonnettes. A few kids were playing out, some on new bikes. Some with toy guns were soon shooting up at me as I stood looking down on them. One lad who had put about forty holes in me shouted up: "You're dead mister."

"No I'm not, you missed."

He then, with greater determination, aimed the gun directly at me and started shooting.

I fell onto the railings and made out he'd got me. Peaking through my fingers, I saw him blow the end of the gun barrel as if to blow the smoke away from the caps that had cracked when he pulled the trigger. He slipped the gun into its holster, turned and then started shooting at anyone else who might be in his line of fire. "There'll be no-one left by the time he's finished," I thought.

Away he went, firing the gun at everyone near him. Passers-by put their hands on their chests, just like they had been shot; someone else fell near a car and cried out: "You got me partner!" The lad was by now laughing his head off at all this sillyness.

I was just about half turned to go back into the house when I heard a voice shout: "Merry Christmas!" I turned back to see who was calling. Below me I saw a chap who was very shabbily dressed, like a tramp.

"Oh yes," I called back to him, "Merry Christmas!"

He waved his hand up towards me in a friendly gesture.

"Who are you talking to?," Mom called at me through the open kitchen window.

"A chap downstairs."

"Who?"

"I don't know, just someone passing."

"Where is he?," Mom asked me.

"He's just passing Mr. and Mrs. Smith's."

"Tell him to hang on."

I called to him: "Hey mister, hang on."

He stopped. By this time Mom had come out on to the balcony. "Hang on," she said. "Hang on."

She disappeared back into the house. The next thing I knew was that Sheila had come out, followed by Mom and Dad. Then Dad went down the two flights of stairs and started talking to the old chap. My Mom went back into the kitchen, dinner still not ready but getting closer by the minute. Dad was still talking to the old man. Then they shook hands and he followed Dad up the stairs and into the house. Dad took his coat and hung it up, then beckoned him into the living room. The old chap followed Dad, we followed the old chap.

By this time Mom had speedily done three jobs: put all the presents away neat and tidy, put the kettle on for a nice cup of tea - and set another place for dinner. This was no surprise to us. Down in the old house in Aston she was always first up the front. Any kids hurt, she'd be there, anybody in need, Mom would be first with a helping hand, a neighbour or friend in hospital, she'd be there with the fruit and the latest gossip.

Tea up. The old chap put both hands around the cup. "Cor thanks Missus, that's real nice of ya." He drank the tea slowly.

"Dinner time," called Mom through the serving hatch. The old chap first, Dad next, Sheila, then me. Mom brought hers out with her. The old chap spoke only to say that the house and the trimmings looked nice and to thank Mom for the Christmas dinner.

The dinner went down a treat, the plates were cleared away and out came the Christmas pud, plus a tin of cream, plus Dad who hid an old tanner somewhere inside the pud. There was jelly or blanc-mage if we wanted it - our Sheila tried everything on offer.

The old chap was very quiet. He just sat there eating and saying thank-you. We all pulled a cracker with him and he put a paper hat on his head.

The sweet finished, Mom cleared the leftovers away to the fridge while Sheila and I helped clear away all the pots, pans and dishes. It seemed to take hours but in fact took only about 15 minutes. Time now to watch a bit of telly, just for the evening news.

Dad was having a chat with the old man. He had given him a good measure of whisky and you could see the old lad really was enjoying the day's celebrations.

After the news it was time to play a few games. The old chap looked on and occasionally smiled at the silly tricks we got up to. Another whisky and he asked Mom if he could use the lav. Dad showed him the way while Mom popped into the kitchen and fixed him up a couple of sandwiches and some cakes. Dad got a large bottle of Nutbrown ale and wrapped it up in some Christmas paper from one of the presents.

The old lad returned. He thanked Mom and Dad and said he hoped we enjoyed the rest of Christmas Day. He shook Dad's hand and followed him to get his overcoat. Mom gave him the sandwiches, Dad slipped him the bottle of ale and he went off down the stairs shouting "God bless you!"

We stood, silently watching as he waved a final goodbye and disappeared into the freezing cold night.

"Brrr. It's gone colder," Mom said as she shuddered. "Let's get back inside and finish our present opening."

"Good idea Joan," Dad agreed.

Sheila stood looking at me. Then, touching my shoulder, she said in a low voice, "Come on Al, he'll be okay. Those people of the road have someone watching over them."

She turned and went back into the house, leaving the front door just on the catch. The old gent had now gone out of sight. I took one last look and followed her.

I locked the door behind me, pulling the top and bottom bolts across, placed the door key out of reach and then went into the warm living room. Mom had poured herself a large gin and tonic, Dad a large glass of beer and two pops were waiting for Sheila and me.

For some time we all sat there just quietly drinking, deep in thought, no-one saying a word.

Then Dad flicked his head to one side, trying to draw my attention towards the kitchen. I casually nodded, left my seat and walked into the kitchen with him.

"I have your mom's big present upstairs and I want you to keep her from coming up while I get it. It's something really nice. When I cough, get her to stand up and close her eyes," he said.

"Okay yes, right Dad, got it," I said.

Dad went upstairs. I think Mom had an idea something was going on but she didn't say anything to spoil the moment. Then Dad started coughing. Sheila started laughing.

"Bad cough you've got there, Bill," Mom shouted.

"Stand up, Mom. Stand up and close your eyes," I said.

Mom did as she was told and Dad came into the room with this full length ladies' top coat, one with a black fur collar, a real smasher. Mom opened her eyes and a broad smile spread right across her face.

"Try it, try it on," Dad said with excitement in his voice. Mom took off her cardy, then just like a class lady she eased the coat on. Well, she looked a million dollars, like someone out of a movie. Dad, Sheila and myself just stood there in awe.

"You look great, our Mom," Sheila told her. "Yes, you're the best Mom in all the world."

"Well, our Mom, nip upstairs and take a look in the full mirror," I said.

"That's a good idea son," Dad said.

We all followed Mom upstairs for this exhibition. Talk about hanging it out. First she turned this way, then that way, this side, then again a turn round this way.

"Oh thankyou Billy," she cried. "That's the nicest present yet." She gave Dad a kiss.

"Hey-up!," Sheila and I shouted together.

One by one we trailed back downstairs, except Mom. Dad headed straight for his pint and we went for our pop - very thirsty work this fashion business you know.

We heard Mom call out for Dad to close his eyes.

"Oh blimey," I thought. "Here we go again."

Dad put both his hands over his eyes. I thought we were supposed to be the kids around here.

I could tell by the expression on his face that he had no idea what Mom was holding up as she entered the living room. It was a three-piece suit, dark blue with turnups on the trousers. My dad's face lit up like Blackpool illuminations. The little man was as pleased as punch. He shot upstairs to try it on. After a few minutes he returned and, well, words fail me. What with Mom in her coat and Dad his brand new suit on, they looked a real pair of toffs about to step out on the town. At that moment, Mom put her hand into her coat pocket.

"What's this?," she said, pulling out another small present Dad had not told her about. It was a lighter, a silver Ronson to boot.

Mom asked Sheila to fetch her a bottle of gin from the kitchen. She came back to find that Mom and Dad had bought her a red three quarter coat with matching bonnet, and some matching gloves threaded to the sleaves so they wouldn't get lost.

Now for another fashion show. Sheila turned and twisted this way, that way and the coat was cut so it swung as she turned. On went the bonnet, the gloves pulled up on each hand and did she look a picture, just like a doll. Mom and Dad were very proud of her, in their smiles were written a thousand words.

I began to wonder what awaited me. I had just got some new clothes, including a knee-length coat which Mom bought for school and the bad weather which we knew was on the way. I asked Mom which room I should disappear into.

She looked across at me and asked: "How do you know you're getting anymore presents?"

"I know you, Mom, and I know that you would never leave me out."

"Don't wanna put any of your dosh on that, do you?," she said.

"Ermm, no Mom. I've not got to the bottom of my stocking yet. Don't really know how much dosh I have."

"More than me," Dad quipped.

"No Dad, no-one's got more money than you."

Mom sat there grinning like a Cheshire cat. "Good old Mom," I said. "What's next?"

Dad left the room and went upstairs. When he came back down, he knocked on the door. Mom jumped up and let him in.

"Close your eyes," they said. "And no peeping, or you'll get nowt."

I put both hands over my eyes so as not to peak through. Imagine me going through this rigmeroll at thirteen. Well I had to join in or no prezzy. The first present I was given was by Mom.

"Open your eyes," she said. On the table in front of me was this square looking object all wrapped up in bright blue Christmas paper which was securely fastened down with sellotape to prevent pre-Christmas peeping.

I was very excited at the thought of what it could be. I felt one side, then ran my hands over it but it was the same all round, just a square. Finally, I had to open it. It was three large blue Eveready batteries. I didn't have a clue. I just stared at them trying to puzzle out what on earth anyone would want to give me batteries for. Then Dad handed me another present. This one was very thin and once again well wrapped up. I tried again to puzzle out what it was. I opened it up and to my total surprise there was a bright red plastic control panel with a knob on the top. It also had two long wires coming from the top and held in place by two small nuts. Another present then followed. Dad passed it over to me saying it was from Uncle Fred. Again, it was firmly wrapped up. I opened it slowly, doing one of Mom's take your time efforts. It was about a foot long and in pieces - a loco shed, beige in colour with a green roof, green drain pipes and lots of nuts and bolts, just like Meccano.

Then Mom handed me another present, a really big one.

"Cor Mom, it must be two foot by three foot, not too heavy though."

Mom looked over and told me not to shake it or tip it up as I might bust it. Very carefully, I opened it. I couldn't believe what I was looking at.

"Wow, a train set," I said. "It's a train set, look everyone." I was so excited I gave Mom and Dad a great sloppy kiss. I opened the box, first out was a small green Southern Region tank engine, No. 31340. Next came four different coloured open wagons, then a brake van and a dozen curved tracks.

I assembled the track into a large circle, Dad wired up the controller and Sheila moved a couple of chairs out of the way. Within minutes we were all set to roll. I switched on the power, Dad turned the small knob in the direction of the arrow and off went the train. We all sat there for a while watching it go round and round.

"Look at the time," said Mom. "It's gone ten. The day's gone very quickly, you'll have to wait a year for another like it."

Dad commented that it had been a grand day and then we all thanked each other for helping out over the year. Dad said that he hoped we had all got what we wanted. The train was still running round the room.

"We'll help you tidy up now Mom," I said. I switched off the power controller, untied the wires and put the train set away neat and tidy in my bedroom. We all helped out and the room was back to normal in no time.

Sheila and I took it in turns to get ready for bed. We gave the folks a good-night kiss and then went to our beds. I was just pulling the sheets and blankets up to my head when I remembered the old chap. "I wonder where he is now," I thought. "I wonder if he's alright."

I fell asleep thinking about him - who was he, where did he come from, where did he go?

The next few days passed slowly - not a lot to do; assembled the loco shed Fred had got me, ran my train set and celebrated the arrival of 1963. Due back in school on Monday 7th January. The holidays were great but they could drag on a bit at times, especially with this weather when you couldn't get out much. On New Year's Eve I even tidied up my bedroom, just to pass the time away.

A trip out was needed, just to get out of the house for an hour or two but I didn't want to go very far so it would have to be somewhere local.

"Tyseley on Saturday," I said to myself, looking through my loco book. "Yes, that's where I'll be off to. Now a trip for Sunday." Again I looked in my book. "Kidderminster and Stourbridge Junction sheds. I've never been to them yet, only passed them en-route somewhere else."

It was well after Saturday dinner time when I set off for Tyseley. I took a steady walk up to Six Ways, then the number 8 bus and another walk to the shed. On my arrival it seemed unusually quiet, with a sort of stillness about the place. Maybe it was the time of day, a lot of locos were off the shed out working.

Standing on each turntable, I wrote down the loco numbers in my pad. There were only 40 engines on shed and I copped just four - poor.

I got round and out again without anyone noticing me which was how I liked it. I was never afraid of being caught but this visit reminded me of the time when Melvin, David and I had just bunked a shed and were stopped by the foreman on our way out. He asked us where we had been. Melvin did most of the talking when need be. He said that we had very quietly, safely and very very carefully been round his shed and he spoke with such soft-ness in his words that the foreman just stood there, speachless. Eventually, he said: "So you just ghosted in, then ghosted out without asking me?"

Melvin thought quickly and answered him saying: "We did not wish to dis-turb you."

The foreman looked at us, then said: "You're all quite fearless aren't you? Just for engines." He muttered again: "Just for a few engine numbers."

Shaking his head, he walked us out of his shed. We said we were sorry and promised that if and when we returned we would come and ask his per-mission first. He half smiled at the thought of us actually asking him the next time - "Hello mister, can we do your shed?"

I was alerted by the sound of someone coming up close behind me. I turned round and a driver was ringing the bell on his bike as I was standing in the pathway.

"You'll get yourself knocked over," he said as he passed by me.

"Sorry mister," I shouted after him. Coming back to the present, I headed off for the No.8 bus home.

Sunday morning I was up early and off via Snow Hill to Kidderminster, a nice little shed, 15 steam locos on and one Class 08 diesel shunter. I copped 12, not bad for this little shed. Then I got the train back to Stourbridge Junction. This was a real good shed, 47 on and not a diesel in sight - now that's a real novelty. I was well pleased -copped just under half, 23.

On the bus home, I thought about the trips to come - especially the one we had planned to Cardiff and Swansea - and about the sheds we had done. We didn't actually know much about them, our sole objective was to get in, get the numbers, get out again and get on to the next shed. We never knew how many tracks a shed had, how many turntables or what the coaling tower was like. These sort of statistics were for real railway enthusiasts, not your real train spotter.

Of all our local engines, Wolverhampton Stafford Road's Kings were the ones we loved the most. With its number hidden by the big board on the front, one steams through Wolverhampton Low Level station. *(Arthur Chester)*

THE NEWPORT INCIDENT

The first day back at school was horrible, not many of us wanted to be there and some of the kids in our class never made it in. I bet the school board man got fed up with knocking on all the same people's doors, then having to drink all those cups of tea while listening to reasons why little Johnny, Tommy or Peter couldn't get to school.

No-one was snowballing in the playground, the snow that once lay in plenty had turned to icy patches. It was more dangerous now - for one thing it was slippery but, secondly, everywhere you walked you were hit by people sliding in every possible direction. The front playground was on a rise from the classrooms down to a brick wall so it was great fun to slide down the slope. The fun only lasted until you fell headlong over those boys who decided to race everyone else in whatever direction took their fancy. There was many a human pile-up.

I tried very hard to avoid this playground madness in my efforts to find David and Melvin. We always met up by the corridor entrance; it was a quiet place, away from the playground flyers where we could talk.

David was always in school early, I was always second in and Melvin always third. Melvin, with his round, cheerful face was a bubbly, happy sort of fellow, his gingery hair was wavy and thrown backwards. Chubby in appearance, he always wore a colourful jumper to keep him warm, and an old chequered jacket that he travelled so many miles in. Come rain, shine or snow, he always wore the same buttoned coat. David was very small, a whippet sort of a lad, very quick to move off. No matter how many times he combed his fair hair backwards it always fell forwards.

I found them in our usual place and after going over what each of us had got for Christmas I asked if we were planning a trip for Sunday. Melvin was slow to answer and I took that as a no. I remembered him saying before the break that we might not go anywhere for a while and that Cardiff would be the next. We hoped that as the week passed he would change his mind but he didn't.

On Friday I was approached by a lad who told me that he had seen Melvin just before Christmas, up town and at New Street station. He said that Melvin was train spotting with some older looking lads. I asked him if he knew the lads - were they from our school? He said that they were older than schoolboys, about 16 or 17. One looked older than the rest, at least 20-ish.

From that moment I felt that the pleasure of each other's company that we had enjoyed ever since our first trip to Snow Hill and Tyseley was coming to an end. I went home feeling empty. "Who were these lads?," I thought to myself. Maybe they were just lads who lived near him, or someone he was just talking to but I thought the worst and time would prove me right.

That evening I had a surprise visitor when Tony 'Spinner' Jones called for me and asked if I was still loco spotting. I told him I was.

He said that he had seen Gerry Williams and they both would like to come along on some trips now and then. Also, he had asked Eamon Crawley from along the block if he wanted to come with us, and the Smith brothers - John, Martin and little Kevin - might also come now and then. I went along the landing with Tony just to call and see Eamon's mother. She was a nice Irish lady, pleasant, friendly and always very helpful. She said that as Eamon suffered with asthma, he could only go on local trips to begin with. We then called on Mr. and Mrs. Smith to ask if their boys could come with us.

As Spinner and I parted company he said he would see Gerry and let him know when we could get together at someone's house to arrange some local trips and take it from there.

It was Friday night and I started thinking that I should go on a trip this weekend. I got out my books, timetable and a map of the railway and start-ed looking for somewhere to go. I had to consider the dosh as well - I did have a few quid saved up plus some Christmas money in notes tucked under my mattress - I only counted it when no-one was around to see me. I had a few bob in my money tin as well so, yes, I could go on a good one. I decided on Newport, South Wales. I had never been down that part of the country and so I would hopefully cop a good few. There are two sheds there, plus the shed at Severn Tunnel Junction which I could do if it looked good on the way past.

I packed my rucksack with all the usual requirements - Locoshed book and directory, four different coloured pens, ruler, Western Region timetable, eggy-loo sandwiches, pop and a packet of JDs. My clothes were getting all nice and warm in the airing cupboard, coat and scarf too. Now to bed for a good night's sleep - must be up early tomorrow.

I was very excited at the thought of what I would be doing the next day, all the new locos I'd see in Newport plus all the sheds I'd be passing on the way. I seemd to spend hours tossing and turning, trying to get comfortable but I must have dropped off eventually. The next thing I knew Mom was calling me to get up.

The bathroom first - a quick swill - clothes on and downstairs for break-fast. On the way downstairs I asked Mom if she wanted a cuppa.

"No thankyou," she replied. "Just get yourself ready and be careful down there."

"Okay," I said.

"What time will you be home?," she called after me.

"Oh, it'll be after teatime, about six or seven. See how the sheds are en-route, might stop and do some extra if they look full."

"Alright, and go careful," she said again.

A bowl of hot porridge, a couple of rounds of toast, mug of tea and a quick check of my bag, coat on and I was out the door going for the bus to town.

At Snow Hill, a DMU to Newport was waiting in the platform. It was nice and warm but full of diesel fumes, first thing in the morning too.

"Cor," I thought. "Fancy working on one of these all day and every day, it must be bad for you." I could feel my throat getting dry and could taste the fumes in my mouth.

The unit eased its way out of the bay. "I'm off," I thought. Pad out and at the ready, windows on both sides cleaned with paper towels from the toilet. The train travelled down via Stourbridge, Kidderminster, Worcester, Cheltenham, Gloucester and Severn Tunnel Junction. This shed did look very good and I resolved to do it on the way back.

As soon as the train arrived in Newport I pulled out the directory and found a bus that would take me to 86A, Ebbw Junction shed. The journey took a while but as it was a Sunday not many people caught the bus. I explained to the conductor that I had never been here before and could he please tell me when I'm at the stop for the shed.

"Here we are," he said as the bus came to the end of a muddy path leading to the shed entrance. I decided not to follow the path but to save some time by taking a short cut across an open area of snow-covered grass. This was a big mistake.

I had only walked about four or five yards when the ground beneath my feet left me and I dropped with a jolt as the rucksack on my back jammed against the side of whatever it was I had fallen into. I spread out both my arms which held my body up, then I started to kick, at first with the toe of my right foot, into the side of this hole. My Mom's half-pointed black boots came to the rescue and I was able to make a foothold in the mud which had been softened by the snow. I then kicked with my left foot, trying to hold myself up, hoping that by kicking my feet I could make some sort of step to balance on.

I had been there for what seemed like hours - about fifteen minutes actually - when I heard the wheels of a bicycle slowly approaching me.

"Help!," I called out. "Help me, I'm stuck. Over here!" Turning very carefully and slowly to my right hand side, I could see a railwayman coming along the path. He was totally unaware that anyone was here.

"Help! Help!," I called out again, in desperation. "I'm over here, look!"

The man stopped, tilted his bike at an angle on the path then approached me. "What are you doing there?," he asked.

"I fell down this hole. Can you get me out?," I asked him.

"Let's see, what's below you?," he asked.

"I can't feel any ground but my arms are starting to hurt me," I answered, "and the rucksack is the only thing that's keeping me from falling further down. Please, please get me out, it's hurting even more now."

The man moved very cautiously, step by step, towards me.

"Stop!," I cried. "Look at where my footprints are in the snow, that part of the ground is safe to walk on."

He looked down and said: "That's a good idea, good."

One foot in front of the other, he slowly edged his way towards me and was soon standing just behind me. For a moment he looked to be studying the situation.

There was another jolt and I felt my rucksack shift up to the back of my neck as I dropped a little further into the hole. My arms were now inclined upwards as well as outwards and were hurting more than ever. I was very frightened.

"Please, please help me," I cried.

"Okay son, don't worry, you'll be okay." said the railwayman. He asked if the straps on my bag could be undone.

"Yes," I said.

"Right," he said, "we will undo them one by one then I will take the bag in one hand and hold you as I take it with the other hand."

This took about five minutes but it felt like an hour. I breathed in as much as I could to give him some room to get the bag out, I could feel it moving away from my back as his hand grabbed hold of me. Then he changed hands and the bag was free. He asked me to help him by pushing myself against the wall of the hole which would make it easier for him to lift me out. I did this and I was at last out of the hole.

We walked back to the path. He carried my bag and asked: "Are you alright?"

"I think so," I said, "just hurting a bit from holding myself up."

"Look at the state of your clothes." He pointed to the mud all over my trousers and boots.

"Come on, you just stick with me," he said. He pushed his bike all the way to the shed. I followed close behind. I had been too smart for my own good and this short cut had proved to be a long cut.

We arrived at the shed foreman's office. He looked at me all messed up, spoke a few words to the railwayman and then suggested I go and stand near the coal fire to try and dry off.

A few minutes passed then he came over with some cloths for me to clean my boots with, and then he found a clothes brush for me to brush the mud off with once it had been dried by the heat of the fire.

I must have spent over an hour at this shed and not a single number had gone in my pad yet, and there was another shed to get to, plus Severn

Tunnel Junction.

"I'll be here all day," I thought to myself but I had to be careful not to upset anyone as they really were trying to help me out of the mess I had got myself into. Best enjoy the warm fire, get dried and make my way off the shed.

A chap arrived with a nice cup of tea. I thanked him and thought about a sandwich while I got dry. Some time later the foreman came back in and asked me if I was okay. I said yes and thanked him for helping me to get cleaned up. He then asked me what I was doing at his shed. I explained that I had come all the way from Birmingham to do his shed - with his permission, of course. He eyed me with a "I've heard that one before" look.

"You must hang on here," he told me. "Don't go off anywhere, okay."

"No," I replied, "I'm not going anywhere."

I thought, "This is it, I'm in trouble now. He'll be getting the police. Great, all I need now is for the police to come for me."

The foreman returned a few minutes later with another railway worker. "Go with him," the foreman said.

I put my half eaten sandwich away, tidied myself up and said thankyou to the foreman once again, then closely followed the other chap. He handed me a piece of paper and said: "Just stick close by me and look at the paper later on, but don't do it now, okay?"

I slipped the paper into my inside coat pocket as he led me a quick trip round the shed and the yard outside. There was a good selection of locos on but, as instructed, I never wrote any of them down.

Eventually we came to a small car which was a little on the dirty side. "Hop in," this chap said to me. For a moment I wondered why he wanted me to get in his car.

"It's alright," he said. "You're not in any trouble and you do want to get to the other shed, don't you?"

"How did you know I wanted to go anywhere?," I asked him.

"I used to collect engine numbers just like you and if you've followed your directory this will be the first shed you've come to visit. Am I right?," he asked me, smiling.

I was about to answer when he said that the difference between him and me was that he would not have fallen down a hole. I looked at him and then started to laugh.

I sat in the passenger seat and placed my bag across my knees. The car started up and we left down the long drive and headed off towards the second shed, 86B, Newport Pill. We were heading towards the docks and going a bit fast for some reason which had me rather worried.

Nevertheless, we arrived safely at 86B. He parked the car and we both walked in the direction of the shed.

"This way," he called. I followed him, not having a clue where we were going.

"Stop here," he instructed me.

I stopped there and stood looking at the locos that were around the yard and shed area. He returned and advised me to follow him around the shed. We took about ten minutes then he said: "Back to the office."

He went inside the shed for a second time, then suddenly he reappeared and said we should leave. He drove me to the station and when we got there he gave me another piece of paper.

"On your way home, write down the loco numbers that are on the two pieces of paper," he said.

I said thanks, opened the car door and had a quick look at my watch. The train I was due to catch to Severn Tunnel Junction would soon be in. I waved goodbye as he pulled away.

I headed off on another diesel unit to Severn Tunnel Junction, feeling a real mess with mud caked on my boots, my coat and my trousers, and glad to be going home after this shed. The train arrived, I was quickly off and following the directory to the shed. All I wanted to do was get in and out again and be on my way home to Birmingham.

The daylight was fading by the time I got back to the station. The platform lights came on, intensifying the cold, misty atmosphere. I felt chilled and a bit on the miserable side. One or two engines were knocking about in the yard opposite the station.

A train pulled in going in the opposite direction to me, then some people arrived on the same platform as me and a Bristol train was announced. Even after my privations, I found myself thinking about catching this train and doing the Bristol sheds. With only a minute before the train pulled in, I had to think fast. "No, I'll get off home," I decided.

The Bristol train left and I stood there waiting for mine. Only a couple of other passengers remained on the same platform. It was a lonely feeling. The silence of the evening was only punctuated by the sound of goods wagons bumping into each other over in the yard, and a whistle as a train pulled out. Clang, clang, clang, went the wagon buffers, louder and louder as the train picked up speed.

Eventually my train came in - another unit. I found myself a warm spot, rested my head on my rucksack and closed my eyes for what seemed only a few seconds. The next thing I knew, the guard was shaking me and asking for my ticket. I woke up saying: "Errmm, what, what?"

"Ticket, your ticket please," he asked me again.

"Oh er, sorry," I said. "Must have dozed off. Where are we?"

"Cheltenham," he answered. "Where are you going to?," he continued excitedly. "Not Gloucester, I hope, because we've passed it. You'll have to go back."

"No, I'm going to Birmingham," I told him.

"Well, why didn't you say so. I thought you'd gone past your stop," he said.

"No, Birmingham," I told him for the second time.

"Good, then you're on the right train," he concluded.

I took the ticket from my inside pocket, at the same time feeling the pieces of paper the railwayman had given me.

"There you are," I said, handing him the ticket.

He looked at me, then clipped it and gave it back saying: "Don't lose it will you."

"No I won't," I said.

He went back down the train and I got myself comfortable again. These diesel units were awfully smelly but really warm for a sleep. I was next awoken by a steam engine whistle. I looked out the window to find myself in Snow Hill. I stretched, put my rucksack over my shoulder, picked up my pad from the small, half-moon table under the window, made a quick check that nothing had fallen out of my trouser pockets and stepped, half asleep, onto the platform. I made my way wearly up the stairs from platform seven, gave up my ticket at the barrier and made for the bus home and a hot supper.

The bus conductress looked as I stepped onto her bus. "Been scrapping have you, or did you just fall over?," she asked me with a smile across her face.

I looked down at the mud still clinging to my clothes. "No. I just fell down a hole in the middle of a field and if I were to tell you the whole story we would still be here tomorrow."

"Big hole was it?," she then asked.

"I don't know," I replied. "Never had a big enough ruler with me to measure it."

One or two passengers started to laugh on hearing the conversation we were having.

"Mmmm," she murmured. "Mmmm, field you say."

I held my bus fare in my hand and waited for her next comment.

"You can keep it dear," she said. "Your mom will give you a real clout round the earhole, I bet, when you get in. I've never seen so much mud on any one person before."

Again, this caused people to turn their heads and give me another good looking over. Can't wait to get off this bus.

"Just sit there lad," the clippy told me. "I don't want you mucking up my bus with your muddy boots."

"Okay, okay, I'll just sit here on my own with my muddy self," I said. This brought another round of laughter from some of the other passengers.

"Where was this hole son?," one of them asked me.

"Newport, in South Wales," I told him. "And before you ask did I go all the way to South Wales just to fall down a hole, no I didn't."

The passengers were now all laughing at the humour that was being banded around the lower deck of the 33 bus.

"You're pulling our legs, aren't you lad?'," another asked.

"No no. You don't really think I came out of the house like this, do you?"

"Well I've known all sorts of people get on my bus," said the clippy.

This caused further laughter. The upper deck must have been wondering what all the commotion downstairs was about. One passenger shouted down to ask what everyone was laughing at .

The clippy shouted: "A lad has fallen down a hole."

"What hole?," he shouted back.

"A hole in Newport, South Wales."

"Is he alright?"

"Well, he seems to be, apart from being a bit on the muddy side."

The bus finally arrived at my stop in Perry Bar. The banter had stopped but I knew that as soon as I got off, the rib tickling would start up again.

"Mind the step," said the clippy. Then she started laughing at me.

"Keep your eyes open for those holes," someone shouted after me.

"Has he fallen down again?," someone called down from the top deck.

"No, not yet," the clippy shouted back up the stairs.

I smiled at the conductress as the 33 pulled away. She smiled back and I waited for her final smart comment but she just laughed and waved me goodbye.

The next round of questions were to come from my mom so I thought that if I tell her first what had happened, she might not ask too many questions. I thought maybe I could sneak in without being seen and I felt for the front door key hanging on its string inside the letterbox. No good. By this time of night Mom had placed it on the latch, out of reach. I had to ring the bell. Mom came to let me in.

"Thanks Mom," I said. "Cor, am I glad to be home, dinner smells nice."

"I'll put it in the oven and warm it up for you," she said. Walking away from me, she asked how my day had gone.

"Oh fine, fine," I answered.

I took my boots off first, coat next, and left them in the small hallway. I could not leave them where Mom could see them just yet. If she saw them before I had time to explain about the mud I might be in some bother.

Then I thought to myself: "I'll go straight in and tell her the truth as I had been brought up to do."

"All right Mom?," I asked her. "How's your day been, eh? Er, Dad gone down the Crown?"

"Alright, what've you done?," she asked me. "No trouble I hope."

"No, just fell down a small hole while collecting loco numbers at Newport," I said.

"Hurt yourself?," she asked.

"No, got a bit muddy though."

"Come on," she said. "Come and eat your supper up."

Cor, roast beef, mash, carrots, peas and lashings of thick, brown gravy. Just the ticket after a trip out manholing.

"Got some rice pudding for you," Mom told me. "Do you want a drop of milk on it?," she asked.

"Oh yes please," I answered. My dinner went down a treat

"Ill take my crocks into the kitchen for you Mom," I said, "Then wash them up and get myself all ready for bed and school in the morning."

"Okay son," she said. "And when you come home from school tomorrow you can tell me all about your day out and the mud all over my boots and your trousers and coat." She never missed much did our mom.

"Alex, Alex! Come on, school. Time for school," were the words that woke me up on Monday morning.

I never bothered looking out of the window, nothing would have changed. I looked over at my muddy trousers and realised I had no trousers at all to go to school in. I called down to my mom and asked what could I wear for school seeing my trousers were all muddy. A few seconds passed, then she shouted back: "You'll have to wear your jeans just for today."

The thought of wearing jeans to school - oh dear, this was not the ideal way to start off the week. I must get out of this wearing jeans to school. They were the only pair I had, very dark brown with gold sewing in the material and I would look a real twit walking into school in these cowboy jeans. I took them out of the small cupboard and, to my surprise, they were rather grubby. A day off school, I thought - or at least the morning off.

"Mom, mom," I called from the top of the stairs.

She popped her head round and looked up the stairs at me. "I'm trying to get ready for work," she said, "and your sister is trying to get ready for school. Now come on, hurry it up please."

"These jeans are all grubby and I will look a mess at school," I said. I put them on and made my way downstairs.

"Look Mom, I'm sorry for making you late, but these jeans are scruffy." I knew Mom liked me to look clean and tidy for school every day but especially on Monday.

"Okay, okay. Now look here, take your sister to school then come straight home, wash those trousers as best you can, place the clothes horse by the fire and do your best to dry them out, if you can do that for me, and promise to go to school afterwards."

89

"I promise that if they are dry I will go to school after the lunch break at half past one," I said solemnly.

"Do the house work as well for me please, Alex, and I will treat you this weekend," she said.

Treats, I thought. "Yes Mom, I will have the house looking all spic and span, I promise you that."

Mom went off to catch her bus, Sheila was all ready for school so I went back upstairs to get a jumper as it was still bad out there. I did not want to be out long as somebody from school might spot me and say something to someone. I borrowed my mom's old black beret and walked Sheila to school. I left her by the gates, turned quickly and half ran back home.

Once back in the house, I put the latch on, removed the key and got the hot water running to wash my trousers. I got them done and on the clothes horse in front of the fire to dry. Now the housework - my room first. As quick as a flash that was done, into my sister's room, a quick whiz round, that done. I scurried down stairs and turned my trousers on the clothes horse then went into the kitchen for the washing up. After that I had to pause and think what was next - the living room to be vacuumed, then dust down the three-piece suite, dust the TV, turn my trousers again, then get the ironing board out to press them all nice and smart.

Since Mom woke me up I had been running round like a headless chicken. There was so much to do I had not eaten at all so it was time for some breakfast. Shall I have porridge or shall I have jam on toast. No, sugar on toast. I know what I'll have, just for a change - I licked my lips at the thought of treacle on toast.

I put two thick slices of bread under the grill and went to get my books out while the toast was doing. It was just coming up to 11.40-ish. I nipped back into the kitchen just as the toast was getting nice golden brown. I looked in the cupboard for the treacle. Yes, there was just enough left in the tin for me. Now I wanted a pop to wash it down. "Cor, some Dandelion and Burdock, just about a quarter left in the bottle, great stuff. I scoffed the toast then washed it down with the pop. It felt very tasty in my mouth. Now to my pad for yesterday's numbers.

"Oh," I thought. "They're inside my coat pocket." I went in search of my coat which I still hadn't had time to clean yet so this was the next job for me to get out of the way. I had the boots to clean yet, as well.

I sat down for half an hour looking at the numbers from yesterday. The two pieces of paper with the locos on really did look good, must have been well over 200 on both Newport sheds. On Ebbw Junction was a total of 87 steam locos and 17 diesels, on Newport Pill were 18 steam and 18 diesel locos, and on Severn Tunnel Junction, 57 steam locos and just two diesels. Add to that the locos seen en-route - 18 steam, three diesels plus PWM 650, it had been a very good trip apart from the hole situation.

I looked up at the clock. It was time to put my books away, press my trousers and get off to school.

Mr. Davies opened the classroom door and one by one we filed in and sat at our desks waiting for the afternoon register to be called out. Mr. Davies worked his way through the boys' surnames in alphabetical order until the register was completed. He then folded the register, put it on one side, looked up at the class and asked those who had missed the morning to explain why so he could make a note.

"Mr. Scott, thankyou for turning up this afternoon. I'm sure you have a reason for not attending this morning, and I'm equally sure that your class-mates would like to hear your explanation," he said. A few in the class started exchanging information and rumours as to the reason for my absence and Mr. Davies had to call for order as some were getting a bit on the loud and silly side.

"Mr. Scott, we are all very anxiously awaiting your explanation," he said.

I stood up and was about to open my mouth when a boy called out to me: "Mind the hole."

"Don't fall down," another boy shouted out.

"Shhh," said Mr. Davies.

I told Mr. Davies and the class that while I was out on Sunday, I walked across some snow-covered ground and because of the snow I couldn't see the hole that I fell down." I hoped that by telling the truth Mr. Davies would, because he knew I was a decent lad, believe me.

Everbody in the class was now laughing at me, some calling out all sorts of abuse and wise cracks. Mr. Davies was smiling to himself. He took off his half-moon glasses, slowly shook his head, leaned back in his chair and smiled at me.

"That's very interesting Scott," he said. "But what has it got to do with your non-attendance this morning?"

I was still standing. "Because my trousers got muddy and I had nothing else to wear at school."

Mr. Davies finally called for order. "Alright boys, you've had your after-noon's entertainment, now let's get on with the lesson."

When the bell went for afternoon break, it was a signal for all the Mickey-taking to start again and I found myself on the receiving end of another load of friendly abuse from my so-called school chums.

I was looking for David and Melvin and found them just before the bell was about to go for the end of break.

"Hello boys," I said. David started to laugh. Melvin joined in.

"Not funny," I told them. "I could have been in a lot of trouble had it not been for this chap pulling me out." Once again they both started laughing.

"Sorry Al, just the thought of the situation you found yourself in is making us laugh."

"Yes, yes, I know but if it was not for my rucksack jammed against the side of the hole, I could have fallen a lot deeper. I couldn't feel the ground beneath my feet at all. When I was pulled out I had a look down the hole and I couldn't see the bottom." The bell rang before they got round to asking me where I was when I fell down the hole so as the days went by, I expected them coming up and asking me about it, but they never mentioned it again.

We met up after the final school bell on Friday. They said that the trip to Cardiff next week was on but Melvin said he had no plans to go anywhere this Sunday. David was playing football with his team, so no trip for them. I had my own plans to go to Taunton, taking in Bristol on the way.

I said: "Tarrar, see you both on Monday," and watched them go off home. I felt a bit lost for a moment but after thinking about Newport and how I had now done a couple of trips on my own, I thought that this was probably the best time to call it a day. I felt they had got other interests now and good luck to them. I was off on my trips doing the thing I loved and they were away doing the things they enjoyed, and that was the way it went.

Trips to Wales or the South West might include Worcester shed if there was time. Castle 4-6-0 No. 7033 *Hartlebury Castle,* **Black Five No. 44776 and 57xx 0-6-0 pannier tank No. 4664 were among the occupants on 28th August, 1962.**
(Photo by Michael Mensing)

THE COLD WIND OF CHANGE

Taunton station was very busy, the buffet and waiting rooms were full of people keeping out the cold with cups of tea and hot Bovril which they were sipping slowly, to make them last until their trains arrived. I stood as close to the coal fire as I could and waited for the Paddington train to be announced.

I had to change for the Birmingham train at Bristol Temple Meads - I could have waited longer at Taunton and caught my train from there but the extra time at Bristol allowed me to see if any more locos had come on Bath Road shed since I was there earlier.

The train arrived and a Warship class diesel, No. D812, was pulling it to London. I did like the look of these, a sort of happy, chubby look they had. I smuggled my way into a compartment then felt a jolt as we eased out of the station.

"We're off then," a chap said.

"Yes," another agreed.

"Won't be long now," I added. People would say all sorts of things when travelling together, and there was always a storyteller in your compartment. For me the journey was always interesting because of my hobby but someone would start up a conversation on any topic at all to get the most out of the journey. I joined in between the stations and sheds and I really did enjoy some of the stories that were told.

I stood on the platform at Bristol writing down a couple of engines that were not on Bath Road earlier, all the time listening for the train back to Brum to be announced. It was late afternoon by now and I knew that by the time I left Bristol it would be getting dark. It would be about seven by the time I got back home.

The Birmingham train was as packed as ever with people travelling back from their weekends at home or away. I managed to get a seat on the left hand side as the three sheds en-route were all on that side. I tried to sit near the back of the train, usually the very last compartment so that I could enjoy the noise from the bankers that would push us up the Lickey Incline.

When the train came to a stand at Bromsgrove, I decided to stand at the very back with a couple of passengers who had not managed to get seats, to be nearer the bankers that would now push us up the Lickey.

"I'll be standing from here to New Street," I told a passenger. "If you wish to take my seat then please do."

Cases were shuffled from this point to that so I could get to the window and peep out at the banking locos coming up behind. A moody passenger told me to close "that bloody window" as it was freezing cold outside but others wanted to know what I was looking at. I explained and as we set off one or two asked if they could be a party to the observation. I was more than willing to oblige and I could tell by their faces they were getting a real kick out of watching the locos pushing us up the bank.

Puff, puff, puff, puff, harder and harder became the sound of these little tank engines pushing the heavy train up the 1 in 37 gradient - the steepest on any main line in Britain. Sometimes these trains had 12, 13 or even 14 carriages on but no matter what the tonnage these locos pushed and pushed until the whole lot was over the top and well clear of the points.

Once at the top, a whistle sounded from the bankers to indicate that the train was now well over the summit and the train engine acknowledged them with a hoot from its horn. The bankers stopped, whistled and disappeared into the night as we pulled away from them. They would now cross over the points and run back down to Bromsgrove to wait for their next challenge.

The train entered the tunnel approaching New Street and I picked up my rucksack from the clutter of luggage, slung it over my shoulder and prepared to get out at platform seven. Another successful trip was over and this time I had got home all nice and clean into the bargain.

I awoke on Monday morning to the sound of my dad's voice telling my mom that it had snowed very heavily during the night and to take care while she was on her way to work in town. The snow flakes were as big as half Crown pieces. I gazed out of my little bedroom window that overlooked the washing line area just looking at the beautiful white, clean and curved flakes that were floating down from the snow-filled sky.

"Alex, come on son, you'll be late for school if you don't get your skates on," Mom shouted to me. Then she called Sheila down to get ready. "I'm going now. Be careful on the way to school. Sheila, hold Alex's hand across the roads, it's really bad today."

We hadn't got very far on the way to school when we were involved in the art of snowballing, raids were going on all around and it was impossible not to get bombed. It was great fun when you hit someone below the wasteline but not funny if a snowball caught you in a position higher than that. There were rules to snowballing - not to aim at the face or this would cause others to start attacking you from all directions. Another rule was that you must not, under any circumstances, aim snowballs at girls; this again would bring mass reprisals.

We made our way through raging battles from the maisonnettes to my sister's school in Canterbury Road. This was an all-girls school and it was okay for the girls to sling snowballs at each other but not for boys to join in. However, there was no rule against girls throwing snowballs at boys and like the twit I was, I took my sister right to the gates.

This was a big mistake. No sooner had I said tarrar to Sheila than the attacks started. I thought the lads could dish it out but these girls used hard packed ice balls. Any rules of engagement went out of the window and there was no escape for me as these painful missiles rained down, stinging my body, legs and even my head.

I eventually got clear of the war zone and, still in pain, made my way into another raid, this time on the way to my school. No doubt when I got into the playground, there would be another until the bell went.

The master on duty advised all those that still had snowballs in their hands to drop them on the floor and not on someone else's head. He also said that if any boy had ideas of aiming his last snowball in his direction, retribution in the form of the cane would follow. This was the signal for so many snowballs to hit the deck that the whole playground burst into laughter.

Mr. Holdham stood on the stage with his coat off. All four hundred boys stood there too, freezing to death, our breath visibly rising as if from rows of engines at a big shed. It was an unbelievably cold morning and the school heating wasn't having much effect on this big hall. Still, the formalities had to be observed - all smart in jackets and ties for assembly.

The head put on a brave face, pretending it wasn't cold at all. Around him, the teachers stood dithering.

"What a lovely day," he said. This was his way of starting the week off with a bit of fun. The assembled mass tittered in reply - it was too cold to laugh outright.

The weather had got much worse since the overnight snowfall and the days that followed were cold, wet, dull, dark and thoroughly miserable with no sign of any let-up. The week dragged by - we couldn't even get down to Halford Drive where we played football. In fact we couldn't get outdoors for anything in the recreational department which put the school hall under a lot of pressure. It just could not accommodate all the classes that needed to use it instead of being outside.

The rule that everyone must go out into one of the two playgrounds for break time had to be suspended because, with the awful weather, some boys were going down sick and missing school. The hall was being used by many boys who did not want to go out at break time, especially the weaker ones who, deterred by the prospect of snowball raids, could seek refuge there.

Our school never closed during that very bad winter but around the country the weather took its toll. The newspapers were full of stories about unfortunate situations that many folks were finding themselves in, plus many, many animals perishing in the open countryside. Young and old people alike were falling victim to this murderous winter and its unrelenting icy grip on our country. We all knew it would eventually end but we never thought it would last the best part of six months.

The weather couldn't stop our trip to Cardiff though and we met up at Snow Hill station on Sunday morning 27th January, 1963.

We boarded the diesel unit in the bay platform just as I had done two weeks ago for my trip to Newport. I remembered the diesel fumes as I stood on the step to climb in. Again the fumes from the underframe hit with a force that made me feel sick. I never ever liked diesels and I hated these things.

We were all very excited at what the day would bring. I never mentioned Newport or the fact that I was there just two weeks ago, travelling on the same train.

Everything beyond Newport was totally new to all of us. "Right boys, let's keep a sharp look out here on in. I've never been here before," Melvin explained.

At Cardiff the first and most important thing to do was to ascertain the train out to the first shed on our list - 88B Radyr which came before the shed we had all looked forward to bunking - 88A Cardiff Canton.

We caught the local valley service and when we arrived at the shed it was full. Melvin told us that we must whizz round this one and get back to Cardiff.

"That was a great shed," I said to the boys. "Tank engines all over the place."

"Yes," David agreed. "I have never seen so many tank locos on one shed."

"Great shed," Melvin agreed. "Forty six steamers on and only three diesel shunters."

No sooner had the train arrived back in Cardiff, than we were running along the roads with Melvin leading and telling us the way while reading the directory at the same time.

"Come on lads, come on, another shed to do after this one."

We ran and ran all the way to the shed entrance. I was really excited at the thought of all the locos we would find there. We turned left and, still running, landed up a sort of cul-de-sac with a bridge towering above us still to be climbed. My little heart was pounding, my mouth was all dried up and sweat was running down my face and back.

Half way across the bridge we stopped dead, puffing and panting. We could not believe what we saw. No engines - well, hardly. We rested on each other's shoulders for a moment before slowly, and very disappointedly walking the rest of the way across the bridge. This shed we had all looked forward to bunking was virtually empty.

A voice shouted up to us: "All gone boys, all gone now." A railwayman appeared from just behind some coal wagons. "Not here you see, they have all gone to East Dock. The shed's closed now, everything's at East Dock.

"Come on," he said as we stood there shaking our heads. "Come on boys, there are still a few here."

Eleven, that's all there was at this once great shed, One little tank loco, a class 37 and nine Hymeks. We thanked him very half heartedly and trundled away from the shed.

"Look lads," Melvin said, "let's get on to East Dock." He looked at his watch and said: "We don't have much time to waste hanging around here. Come on, let's get the shed bunked. Come on Alex, David come on mate, one more and then its snap and pop time. Alex, you got the JDs?"

It took us a bit longer to get back to the station than it did for us to run to the shed. Outside the station we got a bus to the dock area where this shed was. We wasted no time in getting all numbers down but it was well past dinner time by the time we were back at the station waiting for the train home. There had been a good mixture on East Dock, 48 steam and not a diesel in sight. I finished off a film on Castle loco No. 5097 Sarum Castle.

Darkness descended as we sat in the waiting room for the train home. We were very quiet, each with his own thoughts as we ate our snap and drank our pop. I promised to break out the JDs on the way home.

A railcar rolled in and the passengers got on board. The doors closed behind the last one and with a dull whistle we pulled out of Cardiff General station. The trip home was a sombre one. We only spoke a few words to each other all the way.

I tried to cheer the lads up with the JDs, four to each of us. But we could not hide our disappointment with the Cardiff trip. I asked David: "Did you play for your football team a few weeks ago?"

"Yes, sort of," he replied. "The pitch was very hard so we just had a kick-about for an hour. Some of the lads only played because they were fed up with stopping in all the time."

"Did you do anything special on the last couple of Sundays?," I asked Melvin.

"No, just hung about the house, a few jobs here and there for myself and the folks. I've not really got the interest I used to have," he told us.

"Ah, this bloody weather," David chipped in. "It gets everyone down, every day the same. No wonder we're all fed up. "

"Come on, what shall we do next Sunday?," he continued. " What about a trip to Crewe. Yeah, come on lads, we always have a good trip there. Come on what d'you say, Melv?"

I looked across at Melvin. His face was on the floor with lack of interest. "Yes," I said, "David's right. Let's get a trip worked out. Come on Melv eh, you're the best trip arranger."

I was trying to gee him up but all the effort David and me were to put in was destined to fail.

"London Melv, what about that overnight trip to do all the London sheds we talked about?"

"Yes Alex, you're right. I think that's a great plan for next Saturday night and Sunday," David said very excitedly. David was working really hard at trying to get Melvin out of his mood over the lack of locos on Canton.

Approaching Snow Hill, we got our books picked up and into our pockets, our bags thrown over our shoulders and looked out for anything in the station as the DMU came to a stand in the bay platform.

"Ah well, here we are, home again lads," I said. "Not a bad trip out. At least we did all the sheds, plus the engines at the two big ones will probably be cops for us so let's just say this trip was full of surprises."

David agreed and said it was better than sitting around the house all day with nothing to do and nothing to look forward to but school the next day.

All this time, Melvin hardly said two words. We walked up the stairs towards the exit. As we crossed the circular car park I bumped into Melvin when he stopped short.

He turned round, looked at us and said. "Look lads, I don't really know how to put this but thanks for trying to cheer me up. It's not so much the trip, but for some time now I've wanted to get into some other aspects of this train spotting hobby."

David and I just stood in the cold night air and I knew what was about to come was the end of our trips out. David's head dropped because he knew what was coming as well.

Melvin continued with his parting statement: "Sorry lads," he said, "but this is the last trip for me. I meant to tell you both this morning but I didn't want to spoil the day."

I didn't say anything, just felt a sadness inside. David said that perhaps it was time for us all to call it a day but we should first see how we felt in a couple of weeks, maybe it was just the weather getting us down.

I nodded in agreement. No-one spoke for a while, we all just stood there in silence, each waiting for the other to say something. Then Melvin looked at his watch and said he would see us in school tomorrow, so we all parted company and went home.

My thoughts flashed back to the young lad who told me that he had seen Melvin talking to some other lads at New Street station some time ago, and was this, I thought, the real reason why Melvin had decided to call a halt to our spotting trips. On the way home I thought of a dozen reasons for his change of heart but it made no difference anyway. But for a surprise trip to Swansea, this had been our last day out together.

TROUBLED TIMES IN WIGAN

The weeks that followed the Cardiff trip were mostly taken up with family life, school and trips out on my own. The weather remained the same.

New sheds in new areas were now my priority and this started straight away with a trip to the two sheds in Wigan on Sunday 3rd February - the first of many that I would undertake on my own.

I had never been directly north of Crewe before and, having stopped off there to bunk the North shed, it was well after dinner time when I arrived in Wigan.

I took my ticket out of my coat pocket then, fumbling for the Shed Directory, stood by the station entrance. Ticket clipped and book open, I made my way to shed number one, 27D Wigan. Following the directory, I soon passed another station, this was Wallgate. I turned left just past this station and kept walking until I arrived at the shed. Walking quietly between the rows of engines, I got them all written down and was out and back to North Western station to start all over again. This time I made for the other shed at 8F Spring's Branch. On the way I reflected on the fact that there had been no diesels on Wigan shed.

I arrived at Spring's Branch in complete darkness. Into the yard on my right first, I thought, then into the shed. After this, a quick scamper over to get the locos in the yard a little further away from the shed. Silence was needed because the depot lights were on and I didn't want anyone to notice me.

Numbers all in my pad, it was now time to very quietly slip away under cover of darkness. The long walk back to the station took some time so I was pleased when I finally got there.

I approached the timetable on the wall opposite the ticket office window, just to confirm the time of the train back to Crewe. I'd stood there for a while, checking the Sunday times, when a voice called out from behind the ticket window.

"What train are you catching?," the man asked me.

I turned and looked at him through the window then said: "The 8.15 to Crewe."

"No," he told me, "that train doesn't run."

"But," I told him, pointing to the timetable, that the train to Crewe was at 8.15. "Look, here in red print, it says 8.15, stopping at Warrington. Look, look," I said.

By now he was getting a bit annoyed with me trying to tell him his job. "Look laddy," he said, the tone of his voice becoming more angry. "Look at the side of the train time and then tell me what those initials say."

I stood right up close to the timetable, my nose almost pressing against it, and saw what he was talking about. "Sunday Excepted." Very slowly I turned back to face him. He had a smurky smile on his face.

"Yes, yes, now you've got it." His smile became even wider and he was right, of course.

"Sorry mister," I said.

The smile had now gone from his face. "Okay son," he said. He looked over at the timetable that was hanging up in his office then told me when the next train was - about half three in the morning.

"Half three, half three?," I said. "I've got to be back at school for nine o'clock."

"Sorry lad," he said, "that's the next stopping train to Crewe."

"What about Birmingham?," I asked him

"No no, that's it. That's the only train that's going to Crewe or any other place in your direction," he explained.

I looked up at the clock above the ticket office. It was just past seven. I sat myself down and took out a sandwich, had a drop of pop, then just sat there. I just could not believe it.

The clock had progressed to just after eight when I heard a clanking sound approaching. I jumped up, grabbed all my stuff and ran towards the platform. Just then a Royal Scot class loco, 46160 Queen Victoria's Rifleman, eased into the station and stopped. I could see the driver and fireman dragging the water hose over towards the engine's tender. As the hose disappeared into the tender they were talking about something but I couldn't make out their words. I turned and then noticed the guard coming towards me, carrying a billycan in his left hand. I ran excitedly towards him asking if his train was going to Crewe.

"No son," he said. "It's going to London Euston."

He walked past me. My heart just fell so deeply I started to cry. The tears trickled down my face as I stood there sniffling.

After a minute or so, a voice called me over. I sniffled a few more times then, because I had never carried a handkerchief, started to wipe my eyes and runny nose on my coat sleeve. I looked in the direction the voice was coming from. It was the guard beckoning me to him. I walked slowly over.

"Come on son, don't be afraid." He placed his right arm around my shoulders. "Stuck yeah?"

"Yeah, my mistake," I told him.

"Look, you just stand there and give me a minute okay."

"Yes, okay mister," I said. "I'll stand here."

After a while, he reappeared and advised me to go with him. We walked back to his guard's van and he told me to sit down while he gave the driver the signal to go. The engine whistled and the train started to move with me on board.

"Here you are," said the guard, passing me a mug of tea and a sandwich.

"Cor, thanks," I said. I drank the tea and munched on the corn dog sarny.

"Hungry?," he asked.

"Yes," I answered. I had already eaten some of my snap at the station but I did not wish to refuse his hospitality. Anyway, this was better than sitting on Wigan North Western station until half three in the morning.

As we headed south I heard him muttering the names of the stations we passed through. He wrote down what I thought was the name of each station in a notebook then looked at his watch and wrote down the time as well. We hardly spoke to each other. I only lifted my head up when we passed through a station, just to look at the lights flashing by. The compartment shuddered whenever another train passed in the opposite direction.

"We'll soon be there," he said, looking out of the side window. "Look, see all those bright lights?"

"Yes, I can just make them out. Oh yes, I see them more clearly now. Where are we?," I asked.

"Crewe my boy," he said triumphantly. "We're nearly in Crewe."

Great, I thought to myself. I'm nearly home. Well, in the right direction anyway.

"Now listen to me," he said with a very serious tone in his voice. "As soon as this train almost comes to a stand, get yourself ready to get off."

"Get off, get off the train, yes."

"Yes, you only have a matter of seconds before I give the driver the tip that you're off and he can pick up speed to get us out of the station quickly," explained the guard. "We cannot afford to stop dead as passengers might try to board the train and this will get us all into trouble, you understand me son?"

"Got it," I said. "You can rely on me. I won't let you down, not after all you've done for me," I answered.

The train crept down the platform, he opened his door and I could hear an announcement saying the train was not for public use.

"Now son," he said. "Now, carefully."

I landed on my feet, well onto the platform. A young man, about twenty-odd started walking towards the guard's doorway. The guard was hanging out of his van holding a lamp showing a green light. A sudden whistle and the train picked up speed on its way out past the bright green signal at the end of the platform and into the night. I waved at the guard as his train began to thunder away beyond the platform canopy. It left a trail of thick black smoke as it disappeared. I walked away feeling very special.

As I walked towards the train timetables I felt a hand on my shoulder. I spun round to find an inspector looking at me with some interest.

"You okay son?," he asked.

"Yeah, I'm okay, why?"

"It's okay son," he said. "I'm just making sure you're alright."

"Sorry," I said, "for being sharp with you mister but you frightened me for a second."

"Oh right," the inspector said. "Well I'm sorry too." Then a warm, friendly smile came over his face. "Just stop on this platform," he advised me. "Your train to Birmingham will be in very soon but make sure you listen to the announcer."

"Yeah I will," I replied. "I've had a good day apart from getting stuck in Wigan."

"Yes son, we know all about you. You just hang on here for your train home. "

"Thankyou," I said to him. "Thanks a lot."

He walked off towards his office on the platform. I never gave it a thought at the time - how they all knew about me. My worry was just how late it was and whether my Mom would tell me off for being late home.

The train was duly announced and passengers were appearing from all over the place, most coming out of the buffet, others from the waiting room where there was a real warm coal fire on the go.

For the second time that evening, I was frightened. "This is your train," a voice behind me said. I turned and a railwayman pointed to the train coming in from the north. Within a few seconds it was in and he was escorting me to the guard. I stood by while he had a few words with him but I never heard what was said.

The man got off. "See ya," he said.

"Thanks," I said, "bye."

The guard asked me to stand just inside his van for a second while he saw his train out of the platform. He glanced backwards as the train finally left the platform edge then, closing the door, turned to me.

"How are you?," he asked me in a friendly voice.

To be honest with you," I said, "I'm just grateful for being on this train and on my way home."

"Yeah, I bet," he said. Then he laughed as he said: "You've had a right cold day today, yeah?"

I was feeling a whole lot better in myself by now. The thought that I was on my way home really geed me up.

"Yes, and all this just because I misread the timetable," I said.

"Oh yes, oh yes, easily done," he replied.

"Sit down lad," he said, pointing to a seat opposite him. I could see along the train out of a small window that was to my right, and if I turned the other way, out of another window to my left.

"This is great," I thought to myself. "I've never had a ride in anything like

102

this before." The train stopped at Stafford, then Wolverhampton. I had a look as we entered and left the stations to see if any locos were about but, not wanting to cause any sort of situation, I didn't write anything down.

The train rolled into New Street station. I looked at my watch and it was just around the ten o'clock mark. I told him I was really pleased to be back.

"Okay son, now get yourself off home," he said.

"Yeah I will," I said, "and thanks for everything. Oh yeah, and if you ever come across the other guard tell him Alex said thanks once again."

Back home I was so tired I could barely stand up, didn't even have the energy left to eat the Sunday supper I usually enjoyed so much. Next day I had some explaining to do as to why I was so late home. I told my tale over Monday tea but, somehow, I don't think the folks quite believed me.

Wigan Wallgate shed, 27D, in 1963 with a pair of 2-6-4 tanks and a 4F 0-6-0 present. *(Jack Wild / Stephen Chapman collection)*

THE MAN FROM THE BBC

Crewe station on a wet Sunday afternoon is not a clever sight - even to the most ardent loco spotter. The rain that had never let up all day came down to the track like a depressing curtain between the soot stained platform canopies. Every now and then, it dribbled through a gap in the glass roof and plopped onto the platform, sometimes onto my head, doing nothing for the damp discomfort I had been suffering since going round the sheds.

I was waiting for the train home when a lad came over just to talk about the hobby and as it turned out he lived close by me in Witton.

We got on okay but all we both wanted on this miserable day was to get off home. Suddenly, a train was announced - the Emerald Isle Express - and it duly pulled into the platform. We looked at each other, then nodded in the direction of the waiting express. We got on, sure that it stopped at Stafford where we could get off, bunk the shed and get a bit more wet.

The train pulled gently out of the station, heading south. We waited until we were past the South shed then wandered towards the back to be near a door opposite Stafford shed. But the best laid plans can go wrong and this one did just that as the we sped through Stafford without stopping.

A chap in a pinstripe suit was sat reading in a first class compartment next to where we stood. I tapped on his door then, on opening it, said sorry for bothering him but could he tell us why the train didn't stop at Stafford. He looked up at us, then told us that this train did not stop at Stafford or any other place en-route to Euston.

I closed the door, then turning to this lad I had picked up with asked: "Do you think he's pulling our legs?"

The lad said: "Yeah, he's playing us on."

I tapped on the door for a second time. "Euston, Euston in London you say is our next stop?"

"Yes son, Euston. This is a non-stop express..."

He had not finished telling me the rest of the bad news when I closed the door on him. This lad looked at me, I looked at him, and we both looked at the man in the compartment who was looking up at us.

I thought to myself: "Alex, my boy, you're in big trouble." We moved away from the compartment, had to think up something special to get us out of this mess. We agreed to ask the pinstripe man to help us out by telling the guard when he came round for tickets that he saw us talking to a railway-man who was pointing to this train.

For the third time we tapped on his compartment door. Again I said sorry for the interruption but we had a big big problem and he may just be able to help us. I went over our plan with him, he listened and after some thought agreed to help us. He told us to stand near his compartment so he could, if and when the guard arrived, tell him the story.

The train was now heading towards the Trent Valley. "Tickets please, tickets please." We could hear the guard approaching, a door would open, then silence for a second, then the door would close.

"Tickets please." Again we could hear him getting closer, another door opened, silence once more, then the compartment door slid shut again.

Then he was right on us. We explained our tale to him. He stood listening to each and every word then told us to remain where we stood. He knocked on the first class compartment door, paused, then went in, closing the door behind him. I managed to slip my foot in the door to hold it slightly ajar so that we could listen in. The chap explained that he was a director at the BBC and he upheld our story. We felt much better after that.

I could only make out parts of the conversation but from what I could gather, the man from the BBC had done us proud. The guard thanked him and turned to open the already ajar door. "That chap has told me what he saw and he has backed your story up. Now I'm off to do the tickets. You two boys stop here and wait for me to come back," he said.

"Yes," we answered, thanking him for his understanding of our problem. He went about his duties clipping the tickets.

The man from the BBC beckoned us into his compartment. We knocked on the door again and slowly entered.

To our surprise, he asked if we had eaten. Our first response was to say no. He stood up, pulled his jacket back with his left hand and with his right hand produced a large dark brown wallet from his inside pocket. He reached inside and took out a ten bob note.

I was closest to him and for a while I hesitated, saying he had helped us enough. He pushed the note towards my hand. "Take it," he said. "You'll be hungry and you may get stuck at Euston."

I never thought about being stuck at Euston. I took the note and thanked him, then we sat for a while, waiting for the guard to return.

I looked out the window on my right hand side - for some reason we were just passing Bescot shed. I jumped up and shouted to the lad I was with: "Look, look. Bescot shed!"

We opened the compartment door quickly with excitement and started to write down the locos. Then it dawned on me that we were near Perry Bar.

"I wonder," I said out loud. "I wonder if anyone from our maisonnettes is down at the station collecting loco numbers because of this diversion."

I tore a page from my pad then wrote on it: "Tell Mom and Dad and police caught wrong train. Going to Euston." I wrapped the note round a two bob piece to weigh it down.

I could not believe what I saw when the train went through Perry Bar station. There was Spinner just coming out of the waiting room. I tossed the note towards the platform, it hit him on the chest then dropped to the floor.

Hanging out of the carriage door I shouted: "Read it, read it!"
I kept shouting as the train picked up speed again until the curve in the track rendered Spinner out of sight.

The lad asked me if I saw him pick up the note.

"I think so," I replied. "Yes, yes, I'm sure he did. Spinner lives just along the maisonnettes from me. I'm sure he did."

The train turned left at Aston sheds and we were still writing the locos down when the guard came back into view. We put our pens and pads away, not wanting to get into any more trouble than we were already in. On passing the chap in the first class compartment, the guard gestured with a friendly wave and a smile. The chap waved back to the guard then gave us a thumbs up sign. We waved and followed the guard to his compartment.

The guard ordered us to sit in a compartment next to his, which we did without question. He advised us not to move unless to go to the toilet and to tell him first if we did.

He closed the compartment door, leaving a small gap so that he could hear any noise from us larking about or playing up. We were certainly not going to misbehave and that was a fact. We could be in serious trouble and I for one was not for making matters worse.

The lad and me pooled our snap then shared it out. I had not even had time for any sandwiches or pop, not even opened my JDs.

It was dark when the guard came for us. Just after passing Camden Loco, I looked at my watch. The time was approaching 8.12pm. We came to a stop in Euston station at 8.15 precisely.

The guard looked along the platform as the train ran slowly into the station. Suddenly, he smiled and waved to someone. We had no idea what we were in for. The scene was like an old spy movie - waiting on the platform were three police constables, two top railway officials and two plain clothes detectives.

We were joined by the chap from the first class compartment. The guard introduced him to the detectives and they went off talking to him. One of the policemen was very concerned for us and asked if we were alright. We told him that we were fine and had been well looked after by the guard.

The two officials walked off with the guard which just left the three policemen with this lad and me walking between them. We were taken to the desk sergeant - he was a big fella. We were separated and each asked to tell the different officers our stories. I told it as it happened, I just hoped that the other lad was sticking to the story we made up.

The time was coming up to 9pm and we were put in a cell together. There we found a small rubber ball, the kind that used to be fixed to a bat with a piece of elastic.

We were left in the cell until quarter to ten when a constable came for us. "Come on lads," he said, "the train for Birmingham leaves at tenpast ten."

I asked how they knew we were on that express from Crewe. He explained that a lad on Perry Bar station had told my folks and they had contacted the local police at Canterbury Road police station. They contacted the police at Euston.

We stood watching the policeman as he conducted a conversation with the lady at the ticket barrier. She had a skirt on, a uniform and a small hat which just fitted sweetly on her head.

Then, to our surprise, the policeman came back towards us moaning and swearing under his breath. He mumbled a few more words then said: "Come back with me."

We walked with him back to the police room. The 10.10 train didn't run in winter.

It was now five past ten. We stood there while the desk sergeant talked to his relief, me staring at the floor. The young constable explained why we were still there. I heard the sergeant say in a real mood: "Oh, bloody hell."

He told the constable to put us back in the cell. I asked the time of our next train home. He looked over at me and said: "Ten past one."

"God blimey," I said out loud. "What we gunna do till then?"

The sergeant said: "Get into the cell and behave yourselves for starters." Another three hours cooped up in this clink, and no snap either.

We found the ball again and played footy until we got really fed up. At about half eleven a chap came in with some sandwiches, a bottle of pop each and assorted biscuits. We tucked in and they were a real life saver.

We spent some time looking at how the day's spotting had gone until another policeman came for us at ten to one. He walked us to the sergeant who told us to stay near the guard's compartment and not to try and leave as policemen were in twos on every station from Watford to Birmingham.

I tried not to laugh but couldn't help smiling at the thought of two police men standing by every exit. The sergeant noticed me smiling and asked if I thought he was joking.

"Sorry," I said. "I know you mean it, it's just the way you said it."

He smiled to himself as we said "tarrar." The constable then escorted us to the waiting train and explained the situation to the guard who took us to a reserved compartment.

The train pulled out dead on ten past one. Peeping through the blinds from our darkened compartment, we could see that each station between between Watford and Birmingham did, as the sergeant had warned us, have two policemen watching the exit. They knew which compartment we were in and stared at it all the time the train was in the station.

We arrived in New Street at half past three to be met by more police, railway officials and my mom and dad. They were both pleased and annoyed to see me, Mom went on about how they had been sat in Steel House Lane cop shop for hours.

Outside the station we were directed to a police van and taken straight to the cop shop where we were again separated and asked to tell our story to the desk sergeant. It was close on half past four when we were eventually taken home, in separate cars. I never saw that lad again.

We rolled up outside the maisonnettes at about 5am. My mom made me a cup of tea while Dad sat with me going over what had happened to us. I told the truth and as it happened both Mom and Dad believed me.

I said goodnight, thanked them for coming to town for me and went upstairs to bed. It had never looked so inviting. I just wanted to fall into it and not get up for a week. My clothes felt so heavy as one by one my shoes came off, socks next, jumper, shirt, trousers. I couldn't be bothered with jarmers, just fell into bed and within a few seconds I was dead to the world. I had the next day off school - I was in no position to make it.

Jubilee 4-6-0 No. 45741 *Leinster* from Carlisle Upperby has its smokebox cleaned out over the ashpit at Bescot shed in 1961. *(Photo by A. E. Wort)*

LITTLE KEVIN

There was a bit of a surprise in store for me at school on Tuesday. I was just sitting down for dinner at the table in the school hall when Melvin came over to me. How was it going on the train spotting front, he asked.

"Not too bad," I said. "Ermm, you been doing much?"

"No," he said. "But I've been thinking, we never did go to Swansea after all, did we? Fancy a trip down there this Sunday?"

I hadn't got anything planned but for some reason I didn't want to go to Swansea. A few seconds passed by while my thoughts went back to all the places I had been with Melvin and David in the early 1960s.

"Swansea, you say, Melvin? Well, that sounds a great idea. Look, we are on holiday from Friday and as we have two weeks off why don't we make our arrangements for the Sunday, 7th April. That way we'll have more daylight and may be in a position to do more sheds en route." Melvin listened very intently and said he would talk to David and let me know.

Melvin, always good for his word, contacted me on the last day of school.

"Alex, Alex!" He called me over to him in the rear playground. "That trip out to Swansea is on for that Sunday. We'll meet up as we did for Cardiff at Snow Hill, okay?"

"Okay Melvin. Err, is David coming with us?"

"Yes, he's really looking forward to it. Tell you the truth, so am I as I've never ventured that far down before."

We did the Swansea trip as planned - it was just great to have one more trip out with Melvin and David. Our first shed was 87A Neath Court Sart. I took a photo of David leaning against Castle class loco No. 5051 Earl Bathurst. Our next shed was 87D Swansea East Dock where more photos were taken - Melvin and David stood next to ex-Cardiff Railway saddle tank No. 1338, then myself and David on the running plate of BR Standard class 4 tank No. 80133, then David and Melvin on ex-Powland & Mason saddle-tank No. 1151, and the final photo was of David with 2-8-2T No. 7226.

We did Landore shed where there was just a handful of locos and then set off home, arriving back in Snow Hill about seven or eight.

This was our very last trip, we had about twelve months left at school together but we would never ever go out train spotting again. Sad really, but we were growing up. They were approaching their 15th birthdays and I would be 15 in September.

My time out of school was now being spent mostly with the lads who lived in our maisonnettes - Spinner, Martin and John Smith and their little brother, Kevin, Nicky 'The Bounce' Hand from the flats across the way, and Gerry Williams, who lived over at Stockland Green, in the King's Road.

I had already done a couple of trips out with Spinner - Leamington Spa and Rugby on a Saturday and the following Sunday to Sheffield, Retford, Nottingham and Derby. He was okay; he got his name from the times we went ten pin bowling. He somehow managed to curve the ball at the last minute to make it spin from the outside to the middle of the lane and got many a strike this way. Crowds gathered round our lane just to watch Spinner in action and he received many a round of applause in appreciation of his bowling style.

Nicky was only about twelve and a half but by all accounts he was a reasonably good outside green bowler. He was a little like Melvin in his build, solid looking and straight up in his stature. He didn't really walk as we knew it, but sort of bounced along, hence the nickname which I think he quite liked.

We spent the Easter holidays down at Perry Bar park, taking with us some snap, pop, sweets, biscuits, pens, pads, and bits of paper to write down the loco numbers that passed while we played soccer and generally larked about. We were all to become really good friends during those teenage years.

On Sundays we went down to the TV studios on Aston Cross to get the autographs of pop stars recording a programme called Thank Your Lucky Stars. We tried our best to get in with the audience and if there were any records up for grabs we'd be in on the act. We collected autographs from The Searchers, The Kinks, Freddie and the Dreamers, Brian Pool and the Tremeloes, Billy J. Kramer and the Dakotas, The Springfields, Joe Brown, Lulu, Adam Faith, The Dave Clark Five and The Swingin' Blue Jeans.

On the train spotting front, we spent most Saturdays that summer at Tamworth. Spinner and Eamon came along, sometimes Gerry and Nicky, and Martin with his elder brother John but not Kevin - at around eight or nine, he was too young.

Kevin never stopped pestering his mom and dad about going on a train spotting trip with his two older brothers. Eventually, they caved in and asked me if I minded him coming along.

"No," was my reply, "just so long as he stays close to me and does exactly what he is told.

The hobby was perfectly safe if you used your common sense at all times and kept an eye open for the dangers that lurked in abundance - vigilance was all important at every moment you were bunking a shed, not just on a point of safety but to avoid being caught by the foreman. A size 10 boot could find your bum followed by a few choice words drawing your attention to the fact that this was a place of work, not the local playground where you could come and go at will. Kevin was soon to find out that danger was never far away, especially when wandering round such dangerous places as locomotive depots.

We were only to visit the two large stations in town, just to show little Kevin the ropes, so to speak. When we got to Snow Hill he was so excited that the beams from his smile could have lit up Birmingham for a month. However, as we walked across to New Street, he began pestering us about going to a shed. John told him we were just looking at the trains in the two stations and not going to any sheds. Kevin started playing up, moaning all the time at John and Martin - like a little boy who wanted too much too soon. I finally gave way and told John and Martin that on the way back home we could nip over to Aston sheds. This was to prove a bad move.

As we sat on the wall, harmlessly watching the engines coming and going at Aston, Kevin started begging his brothers to take him round the shed. They told him it was much too dangerous and he had to be content with sitting on the wall. The crying game soon followed this refusal and Kevin became annoying to all and sundry over this shed lark.

I, more than anyone, could understand the attraction of a big shed and to a little boy it must have looked great fun. The coaling tower reached to the sky like a big wheel at the fair, the tracks were just like bowling lanes, the steam locos magical monsters in motion, and their drivers and firemen just little figures poking out of the cab sides. We gave in.

Before long we were off the wall and crossing the tracks. We passed the massive coaling tower where a huge locomotive - 92220 Evening Star, the last steam loco built for British Railways - stood patiently filling its tender.

I let Martin lead off, myself next, Kevin slotted between me and John. We walked along very very carefully, keeping a sharp lookout for anyone who might have noticed us bunking the depot. By the shed we were as quiet as mice, we could have heard a pin drop on the black coal dust and oil that covered the ground. We continued step by step very close to the shed mouth where we came across a deep ash pit. Like a channel of lava from a volcano, it seethed with a cauldron of red hot ashes from the fires dropped by countless engines after their day's work.

One by one we slowly walked towards the shed mouth, feeling the intense heat from the deep disposal pit as we approached it. I advised all three lads to walk round the pit and on no account to get close - and not to even think about trying to be clever and jump across.

I had just edged my way past Martin as we looked back to make sure Kevin was walking round the pit. He did and seemed okay but suddenly, without any warning, he tried to jump across the corner. He slipped, his body turned at an awkward angle and with his arms flailing backwards he began sliding into the deep pit of fire.

Quick as a flash and with my right hand outstretched, I only just managed to grab his little hand, but his body was twisting round and round. Martin desperately clung to his little brother but Kevin was now dangling over the

111

open pit and screaming as the heat seered up to his bare legs.

John was still on the other side of the pit and for a moment or two unable to help. He cried out, begging us to hold on tight to his little brother. Soon he was with us and together the three of us managed to pull Kevin up and out of the pit. I tried to take his shoes off but they were too hot to touch. I ran into the shed looking for some cold water.

A driver who had seen the incident bumped into me on his way to the scene with some cold water. Together we hurried back to Kevin's aid. His two brothers had by then removed his shoes and socks and sat him down near an old oil drum. He was still shocked and crying uncontrollably. The railwayman poured the cold water from a milk bottle over Kevin's knees, legs and feet then hurried away for more. Kevin began to calm down but he was still shaking with fright from his brush with death, or at least the prospect of being disfigured for life.

The driver returned with two bottles of water and some rags. He told Martin to pour some water over the rags and asked me to help place them on Kevin's feet and legs. John was told to tip some water into his brother's shoes to cool them down.

We had been lucky that day. Only the five of us knew anything about what had happened. The railwayman, after doing all he could for Kevin told us he was okay and had not suffered any burns. He assured Kevin that he was okay and told him that he was a good soldier.

"Look lads," he said, "best get yourselves off home now." He asked which way we had bunked into the shed. All at once, we pointed to the very high wall over the Stetchford lines.

"Come on," he said, "I'll take you all back over."

All the time, the railwayman was telling Kevin what a great little chap he was, the toughest kid he'd ever seen. This I'm sure took his mind off the pit.

Once over the track, we climbed the wall - Martin first, John second, me third and then the railwayman passed Kevin down to us. Once on the ground we shouted our thanks to him, he smiled an odd sort of a smile.

We called into the first tuck shop on our way home and clubbed together to buy Kevin some sweets to take his mind off what had happened. We all promised to say nothing to his folks and to keep it our secret. We had been very very lucky, the story could so easily have ended very differently.

The hobby was short lived for Kevin and his brothers and, so far as I know, nothing was ever said of this terrifying incident.

THE TREBLE CHANCE

This Sunday, 24th March, I was indulging myself in a solo trip to London where I intended to do some new sheds.

Arriving at Paddington on the 10 o'clock train from Snow Hill, my first move was to get the tube to Wandsworth Road and Nine Elms shed. Following the directory to the letter with brisk walks interspersed with the occasional trot I was soon at the depot entrance. The shed foreman was sitting in his office. I tapped on his door, he opened it and, looking down at this poor, sad looking lad, asked the obvious question: "What do you want, little lad?"

I looked up at this larger than life gaffer and, trembling a bit, told him that last year the very nice foreman had let me go round his shed.

"Describe him," he asked, interrupting my special plea.

"Well, he had on this long blue cow gown, a bit on the plumpish side, very friendly."

"Ermm," he interrupted me again, "so you've come from where?"

"Beermingham," I mumbled.

"That's a long way to come just for some locos, you know," he said.

"I know," I replied.

"What about your permit?," he followed up.

My head dropped because I thought I was not going to get into this shed today. My mind was also on the fact that he may well feel sorry for me and let me in. I turned, and in doing so lifted up my head a shade and with a sort of stuttering said that I had no permit but did not wish to become a problem to him. I was turning more away from him and his office when he told me to get on in, but to see him before I left the shed to let him know that I was out again safely.

I slipped my way past him and eased my way into the yard, into the old shed, then the new shed followed by a quick whiz round the yard, all written down and back at his office door in less than 15 minutes.

"God," he said. "You're very quick for such a skinny fellow, aren't you."

I smiled at him, thanked him for allowing me round his shed, then we shook hands and parted company.

Standing by the bus stop, I found myself confronted by a whole list of number 77s I could catch according to the directory. Once the bus arrived, I stood back from the platform and asked the conductor how long it would take to get to the next shed, Stewart's Lane. The clippy told me that I could use the bus but the shed was not very far away from where we were standing. He stepped off the bus for a moment and started to explain with all sorts of hand signals exactly where the shed was. Then he stopped dead and said for me to just jump on the bus. I sat near the entrance and after a couple of stops he put me off, saying turn here, then take a turn there and I would be at the shed entrance.

As I approached the shed I could see a mirror high up on a very tall brick wall and by the time I reached the entrance I could see the reason for it. I was confronted for the second time by a railway official; there were a few people standing outside the shed, then a few more began to arrive and, as time went by, even more were turning up. Suddenly, there was a whole load of spotters standing around the shed entrance. A chap was making his way towards the front of all these people who were just like me.

"Aha, a party," I thought.

I was right. It was an organised party and this chap who looked very much older than the oldest lad, had a piece of paper in his hand. It looked from where I was standing like a permit. There was all sorts of shouting and talking going on, people looking for others in the group, people trying to get those who were hanging back and talking into some sort of orderly line up. Me, I just stood there, waiting for something to come out of all this rabble. Time went by and at last a nice queue was formed by this noisy bunch of spotters from God only knows where.

One by one they filed into the open ground near the official's office. On the permit was, no doubt, the number of people in the party. I could not leave it too long in trying to get to talk to the leader, hopefully he may swing it that I could pretend I was with them. This was possible if they were one short of the number shown on the pass. If not, then he might be able to convince the official that the number of people on the list was wrong. The official stood and counted each and every person who eased their way past him. I was last and I could not get to the leader - he was already inside.

I stood there alone as the others walked away from me. He could tell I wasn't with the party and I never tried to make out I was. He looked over his shoulder at the party that was now a good few yards away from him, then he looked straight at me, flicked his head to one side, then flicked it again in a way that told me to hurry and catch up with the others. I walked passed him as he said: "Mingle in, mingle in with them."

This I did and I was in; the doors were locked behind me and I was on my way round this shed I hadn't done before.

I was the last one to leave after the party. I thanked the official then, as they moved off, I slipped away in the opposite direction. My next move was the tube to Seven Sisters and the next shed at 34G Finsbury Park. This was a diesel shed and there were a few on but it didn't take me long to bunk. I never saw a soul, the shed was done and I was on another long tube ride, heading for another shed new to me, 30A Stratford. Once off the train, I followed the directory via a tunnel underneath the main railway lines.

I was just about to emerge from this tunnel when I saw three lads coming towards me. The look of them frightened me a bit but I had nowhere to go so I slowed to a crawl.

"You won't get in," one lad said to me in a roughish voice.

Then another told me there was a railwayman standing just around the corner on the approach side of the sheds. They were spotters and they had come onto the man by accident, well, they never saw he was there until it was too late for them to turn away. I thanked them for the tip-off. As I was almost out of the tunnel, my footsteps slowed to a near standstill then, one step at a time, I emerged into the open. Without sticking my head out too far I noticed on my right a small flight of steps and a hand rail to hold onto. I followed them and moved very quietly in.

I was walking very close to the rails at this point, looking forward then behind myself after each step, then looking all round in case I had been spotted by anyone. I passed a very large building on my left, then just stood there with my mouth open at the view before me.

I had never seen a depot that was so spread out. In all my time train spotting, I had never witnessed so many sheds in one area - there must have been six or seven and locos were all over the place.

I spent a few moments trying to work out where the hell to start. I went into the big shed I was stood next to. There were more diesels then steam locos so I just wrote them all down as I saw them. From one shed to another, out into a yard, back into another shed, another few locos here, some over there and some more over here.

Back at the station, waiting for the train to Liverpool Street, I counted up the number of locos on this unbelievable shed but what a shock it was to find that there were only 109. The vast size of the site made it look like there were a lot more than this. I sat and imagined how many locos must have been there in its heyday.

The train duly arrived and I was being whisked off to Liverpool Street. On my right I passed a mass of carriage sidings. Some steam locos were in there on stock, the smoke from them rising to the sky. I arrived back at Paddington on the tube about five o'clock, by which time the daylight was just starting to to fade. I dashed round the platforms writing down the locos that were on trains waiting to leave for such places as Cardiff, Bristol and, my train home, to Birkenhead.

The day's haul was a good one and I'd successfully bunked three sheds where the odds looked stacked against me. Total number of locos seen: 133 steam and 154 diesel. There was one outstanding loco on Stratford shed, a steam loco No. 39. I looked it up in my book to find it was an ex-Y1 class, original number 68131. According to my book, it was an engineer's depot shunter allocated to Lowestoft, a shed somewhere down in East Anglia that I would never get to.

A WORKING MAN

I left school on the last day before the Easter holidays of 1964 and the following Monday saw me going off into the city centre for my very first job in a factory.

I said my farewells to all the lads in my class, to others who were coming up behind in their classes and to all the teachers. The last two people I bade farewell to, with a tear in my eye and a heavy heart, were Melvin and David. One at a time I put my arms around them. It was a very sad moment but we all tried to act grown up. We exchanged tales of the trips out we had enjoyed the most but all the time it was just a cover to try and cheer each other up. We laughed at the trouble we sometimes got into - and out of - and how many packets of JDs we must have got through. We walked out of the school gates that we had passed through countless times during the last few years. Outside, we all went in our different directions, never to see each other again. No phone numbers, no addresses to keep in touch. We'd been together only for the hobby we shared.

I was very unhappy working in that factory - my foreman was very large, moody and totally bombastic in his attitude to most of the small workforce. He never asked you nicely to do any job, more "Oi, you ......ing do this," or "You lazy ....r, do that."

I put up with this for some time but was becoming increasingly fed up with this man's abuse and went to see the personnel officer, one Mr. Cooke. I explained that I had not been brought up in an environment like this and felt that I could no longer listen to all this swearing and barracking.

I had this conversation with Mr. Cooke on Friday afternoon. He asked me to wait for him in his office first thing on Monday morning, after clocking in at 8 am. This was in late July - the last week before we broke up for two weeks holiday. Come Monday morning, I clocked on, placing my time card in the machine on the wall next to the works notice board and then went to the personnel office. The foreman came over and asked why I was waiting for Mr. Cooke. I never wanted to lie or hide the facts but thought a simple answer would be best.

"Oh, he asked me to report to him as soon as I had clocked on. He never said why," I told the foreman.

He gave me a very hateful look. I watched his mouth open very slowly - I'm sure he was swearing at me under his breath. I was only a whippet of a kid, small and frail, thin as a rake, but I just sat in the chair, at first looking at him then bowing my head and looking at the floor. He mumbled some words as he left the office, the windows rattling as he slammed the door.

Mr. Cooke was the next person to come in. He wished me a good morning. I, standing up, wished him the same.

"Sit down lad," he said, his voice was soft and friendly. "Sit yourself down.

"Now, let's see," he said, looking deep into a large book that he had opened on the desk in front of him. "Okay, righty-ho. You come with me."

We left his office and were just about to walk towards the next floor up when he told me to stand by the stairs and wait for him to return. This I did.

He wasn't much to look at, Mr. Cooke - slim in build, nearly six foot tall, his fair hair going thin but he was a fair, warm sort of person. You could tell he cared about those who worked at the factory and he would help sort out whatever situation came up. The word in the factory was that if anyone could be of assistance, then look no further than Mr. Cooke.

Then, as I stood there, Mr. Cooke turned from a Mr. Nice Guy to a Mr. Don't Mess With Me. He launched the most ferocious attack on our ignorant gaffer. He never let up from the moment he started telling him off about his continued bad language, dirty remarks and insults to the workers, until he'd finished blasting him about the dishing out of unfair jobs.

Everyone stopped work and all the heavy machines were switched off, leaving Mr. Cooke with an abnormally silent environment in which to conduct this dressing down.

The top boss, hearing production suddenly grind to a halt, came out of his office and, like the shopfloor workers, stood and watched, open mouthed, as Mr. Cooke continued his tirade against the unsuspecting foreman.

This one-man war seemed to go on for one hell of a long time and Mr. Cooke was not going to let anything go unsaid. The foreman could do nothing but take everything that Mr. Cooke threw at him, his mouth ajar. Finally, Mr. Cooke ended the reprimand to a raptuous applause from the shopfloor.

The boss called all three of us into his office. He offered Mr. Cooke a chair but the gaffer was asked to stand - this I am sure he did not take to very kindly.

The boss sat looking up at the gaffer and stated that over the years there had been many complaints about his behaviour and his attitude towards the workforce.

"Men are men," the boss reminded him, "and should be treated as such. We are all here to work together as best we can and life should be made as comfortable as possible for all. The conditions are not as I would like them to be but, as you are aware, we will be moving to new premises sometime before Christmas.

"I wish to remind you that we are now leading up towards our well earned two weeks holiday and also we are in business so, please gentlemen, let's forget our differences and get on with the job in hand, then do a little soul searching while on holiday and see if we can't come back refreshed and try harder to get on with each other, and to get on with the jobs that we are here to do." He stood up and offered his outstretched hand in friendship to the gaffer, Bert, who was still standing up.

The gaffer said: "Thankyou sir," shook hands then walked out of the boss's office.

"Thankyou Mr. Cooke," said the boss. Then he looked at me and said, smiling: "I would like to thank you young man for having the courage to speak up for yourself." His head bowed for a second and then, looking at both Mr. Cooke and me, openly admitted that, as the boss, he should have dealt with this ugly problem when it was first brought to his attention some time ago. He slumped into his chair and said he just wanted people to make the effort and get on with each other, for their own benefit and the benefit of the firm. He looked very saddened at what had taken place but the issue was now over.

The boss rose again from his seat and thanked Mr. Cooke, then sat silently as we both turned and left his office, closing the door quietly behind us.

"He does his best for the firm and has tried very hard over the years to get business for all our benefits," Mr. Cooke told me.

The factory machines were back in full swing and everyone was back at work. I was being escorted by Mr. Cooke upstairs to the first floor. He went and spoke to another gaffer while I stood and looked around. It was all very clean and tidy but certain parts of the floor were covered in thick cardboard. One thing that made me smile was that all the women who worked on this floor wore slippers, hence the cardboard on the floor. It seemed very well organised.

I was still standing there when over came Mr. Cooke and this other foreman. Mr. Cooke introduced me to him and I shook his outstretched hand. Mr. Cooke ruffled my hair which, at the time, was a little on the long side.

"He's a decent lad," he told the gaffer, then turned and walked off towards the stairs.

My new gaffer walked me over in full view of some of the workers then, looking at me with a nice smile on his face, said: "Good lad, good lad. Don't let him sh.. on you. I like a person who speaks up not only for himself but who cares about his workmates too. You look after me sonny boy and I'll not let you down, okay?"

"Yes sir, thankyou," I said.

The few months I worked for him before we left for the new premises were very enjoyable, and profitable too. He was a great gaffer, the type you dream about. I was a very fast worker and if we started to fall behind, as we did at times, he always asked me to help get the job out on time, or early. I tried never to let him down, nor those I worked with. The whole set up on the second floor was just everyone for everyone, no real animosity. We all did our best to help each other as best we could. Some leg pulling went on but it was all in a day's work.

I picked up my wages plus my holiday pay in a small sealed brown envelope - thanked the gaffer for the overtime that really boosted my pay packet - and went in to wish Mr. Cooke a very pleasant holiday.

"Same to you, young man," he said.

The next stop was the boss. I knocked on his door, stuck my head round and wished him an enjoyable two weeks off.

"Thankyou, and you look after yourself on holiday too," he said. I was by now feeling on top of the world. I wished everyone on the second floor a nice holiday, and some of the chaps downstairs that I had made friends with.

I was walking out of the factory gate, pay packet tucked away inside my coat pocket, a bounce in my step, the sun shining and thinking "Off to Crewe on Sunday then on the coach with Mom, Dad and Sheila for two weeks in Llandudno" when I saw my old gaffer, Bert, getting into his car. I carried on walking - I wasn't going to let anyone spoil the way I was feeling right now - but then, after a couple more yards, I stopped, turned and walked towards him. My steps quickened as I approached him, by now he was just about into his driving seat.

"Bert, Bert," I called out to him. He knew it was me calling to him, his head was already half turned in my direction as he twisted round in his seat. Without any fear, and without stumbling my words, I wished him a most enjoyable two weeks holiday and stuck my thumb up in his direction. He never spoke, just sat upright in his car. The door closed, I turned and felt a little on the sad side but soon shook it off as his car started to move away.

I was walking in the opposite direction when I heard a car pull up alongside me. It was Bert. He rolled down the window and, looking straight at me, said in very sincere words: "Have a nice holiday yourself, son. Oh, and don't forget to bring me back a stick of rock."

The window halfway back up, he pipped his car horn and pulled away shouting: "Tarrar son, see ya in two weeks time."

He'd gone and I felt really great as I bounced across the road for the bus home.

I always gave my unopened wage packet to my mom. I never opened it. She was always very fair and gave me what I needed. I was still only 15 and my pleasures were simple.

My Sunday trip to Crewe followed the usual course that I had followed so often with Melvin and David. Off the train, over the footbridge into Crewe North shed, then to the works - a few bob in the commissionaire's collecting tin ensured my entry with a visiting party - then off to Gresty Lane and Crewe South.

As usual there was a great selection of locos. At Crewe North an exciting mixture of nine Brits, six Coronations, two Jubilees, a handful of Black Fives, some tanks, a few diesels - type 4s and type 1s. High spot of the works was the string of Brush Type 4s, D1610-32 under construction in the same spot I saw the Westerns being built three years ago. A good few steam locos were still there, including three Brits as well as 9Fs, Black Fives, tanks, Standards, Consuls and a pair of Jubilees. Electric locos included 26016, 26057 and 27006 while among the diesels was a single Co-Bo, number D5719. Sixty one steam locos were on Crewe South plus a couple of Western class diesels. For the whole day I copped 73 - not bad.

When I got back home, the folks were all in and getting ready to go on our hols. I ate my supper smartish then gave a helping hand as required. I got my case all packed - Sheila had had hers packed since this morning; Mom and Dad's was also ready. We were all in bed reasonably early as we had to report to the coach depot at Flight's around nine on Monday morning.

Shows and events were the attraction for Mom and Dad - Sheila liked them too as they gave away nice prizes for the best dressed girl, best hair-do, nobbly knees, lovely legs and all that sort of thing.

As for me, I did plenty of sun bathing, penny finding in the amusement arcades and skirt chasing - my main interest during this holiday.

My mom and dad put no restrictions on what I did or where I went as long as I used some common sense. The dance floors at the clubs and discos were packed with all the trendiest dancers, competitions were a real eye opener but most of the lads were only there for the girls. Mind you, some girls were there to get you and most lads met up with one or two - or six or more.

The last Saturday morning at the coach park was like going off to war or something. Boys and girls were kissing each other goodbye, exchanging addresses and promising to write, holding hands and cuddling. Then, one by one, moms and dads called the romantic proceedings to an end as the coaches prepared to leave for Burnley, Manchester, Liverpool, Birmingham and all points North, South, East and West.

The coaches burst into life and moved off with smiling young faces crowding rear windows to wave goodbye through the diesel fumes.

We arrived home just after four o'clock. Mom rushed off to do the weekend shopping. Sheila and I unpacked, Dad got his and Mom's gear sorted out. The cases were put back in the loft for another year and the tea table all laid out, just a case now of nipping down to the chippy for some fish and chips.

Tea over, I nipped upstairs to make a quick study of the dosh left over from my holiday and to consider my next train spotting trip. "Now let's see,

Manchester? No, Liverpool? No. ermm, tut tut, London? Yes, London," I muttered to myself.

I went back downstairs and asked my folks if I was okay to go to London tomorrow. Mom glanced in Dad's direction, Dad looked across at Mom then they both agreed it was okay.

"Any chance of a few bob then please. Dad, can you spare me a few shillings towards the train fare?," I asked.

My mom sat and said: "I've spent a fortune on holiday and you're asking me for a few bob?"

Another pause. "Well, it's like this, the train fare is...." I knew my mom would stop me going any further into the cost but I carried on for a while "then the tube fare..."

"Now then," she stopped me. "Okay, okay, okay, I've heard enough, a quid and no more."

"Cor, thanks Mom." I gave her a big hug.

Dad started to laugh as it would be his turn next. He stood up and, holding out the palm of his hand, said: "I don't want to hear about any cost of this or that." Putting his hand in his back pocket and taking out his fancy wallet, then turning away from everyone so they could not see how much cash he had on him, he extracted two crisp, brand spanking new pound notes.

I rubbed my hands together at the thought of these notes for my trip to London. But I was a little premature. "Give one to Sheila," he said smiling.

Mom chipped in saying: "That'll wipe the smile off your face, Alex." Dad looked over at Mom, then said with a chuckle: "Oh, by the way Joan, don't forget you now have to give Sheila a quid."

That wiped the smile off Mom's face. We all laughed at this face wiping lark. Sheila jumped up and gave Dad a big silly kiss, then Mom got one and we both had two quid each. Actually, I had a lot more saved upstairs but thought to keep it under my hat - or better still under my mattress - until I needed it for this Sunday.

My next day's trip to London was the very last I would make to that area. I opened my account with the first shed over the River Thames, 73C Hither Green. There were 24 diesels on and I copped 21 - a really good start to the day. Norwood Junction, 75C, was the next shed to be bunked; the steam locos that were once on this shed were no longer there. Instead were 17 diesels, I copped 10. Now over to the next one, 75D Stewart's Lane - don't know why but there were only nine on and I copped just three - the day was starting to go down hill a bit.

Nine Elms, 70A, was the next one to get round. The foreman again spoken to with the same sincerity and courtesy as in the past and that got me in. This was one of the last great steam strongholds on the Southern Region and even here, a few diesels had found their way in. Still, I wrote down 74 locos including nine Merchant Navy class, 17 West Country and Battle of Britain class, some Standards - including a couple of namers - some tanks, a few Q1s and six diesel shunters.

I bade a sad farewell to the Southern side of London and went back across the Thames to my next shed, Old Oak Common. Another fine cross-section of steam and diesel locos - into the first roundhouse, all numbers into my pad, then through the next three, followed by the small workshops and out into the ever stretching yard. I stuck my head into the massive carriage shed, just in case, and then took my time walking up the slope out of the shed, turning a dozen times to look back on yet another great shed that had given me so much pleasure over the years.

I had so much feeling for this hobby, so much concentrated love for these steam locos that it hurt me to look at them knowing deep within myself that I was looking back at history.

I had a few tears in my eyes as I glanced up to see the smoke from the locos in the four roundhouses filtering upwards from the roof ducts towards the clear blue sky. I took one final lingering look back from the top of the slope and felt my hand involuntarily rise to wave in the direction of these soon to be forgotten fire eating machines.

No time to feel sad about their demise. Oh yes there is - a lifetime of sadness for those who came to love these locos, to smell the smoke, to taste it, to feel the heat of the fire as you climbed across the footplate to get from one side of a line of locos to the other, to jump in fear as a jet of steam blew off near you, to hear the shrill of a whistle close by, the feeling on a platform as an express came thundering through - the whole of your body trembling with the shear force of the train passing - the crack of the windows as two trains passed at speed, the bouncing of your body as the train crossed over a junction, the sound of the wheels clattering over the points, the wheeltapper's hammer ringing against the carriage wheels as your train stood in the station, and the clang of wagons being shunted in distant marshalling yards. This was now the age of Beeching and not only were my beloved steam engines on their way out but all these sights and sounds that brought me so much pleasure were under threat.

One last sniffle - my coat sleeve had seen better days so I wiped my nose and eyes on it and headed off down the road towards the last big shed on my list - 1A Willesden.

I slipped quietly round this large freight depot with its mixture of locos - exactly a hundred on - and then made my way back to the tube station at Willesden Junction.

The walk back to the station was taken with a more leisurely stride than the usual hundred mile an hour dash. As I stood on the platform waiting for the train back to Euston, a couple of passenger trains flew by, then a whistle rang out from the shed - another engine was moving around getting ready for its next duty. Trains were passing overhead on the high level - a very busy area, Willesden.

Euston checked over, a quick look at my watch and it was time to make my way over to Paddington for the train home. Paddington was a hive of activity, people all over the place, trains coming and going in all directions. I did a quick whiz round the platforms before getting into my train. I found a nice cool compartment, a table already set up, out with some well-earned scoff, books, pad, pop and whole packet of JDs to myself.

After Reading came a chance for me to check my pad and books to see how successful the day had been. Forty five steam on Old Oak Common - some Castles, a few Granges, some tanks, a single 9F but the steam locos were just pipped by the diesels which numbered 47 - shunters, Warships, Westerns, Hymeks and no less than 13 class 47s. Seventy two steam locos were on Willesden including eight Black Fives, three Jubs, one Scot, two Coronations, eleven Brits, three 9Fs, a few Standards, some tanks and quite a number of Consuls. The 28 diesels included the Co-Co No. 10001.

"Another grand day out," I thought out loud. Total number of steam locos seen was 204. But, wait a minute, I only copped 25. I fared little better in the diesels department - 173 seen, 64 copped.

Still, it was a worthwhile catch altogether and my love for this hobby was in no way diluted. After I gave up train spotting, no other hobby would give me anywhere near as much enjoyment, not even football, cricket, fishing or tennis - none of them drove me in the same way as the desire to get out on a train and see the towns and cities passing by.

Monday morning, up early and my first day back at work after the hols. Clocked in nice and early then went looking for Bert with two sticks of rock wrapped up in a brown paper bag.

I saw him talking with one of the workers, waited for my moment then went over to him. A Monday morning smile on my face and a bounce in my shoes, I said: "Good morning Bert. How did the holiday go?"

"Ah, young Scott. Well, me and the wife had a grand time, weather fabulous, food as good and the beer very much to my liking."

I smiled at his report and quipped: "So you had a good time?"

"Yeah, how about you?," he asked me.

"Really great, plenty of what you had, well not so much of the beer, more in the way of shandy."

We stood talking for a few minutes then I gave him the sticks of rock that he, in jest, had asked me to get him.

"What's this?," he asked, taking them from my hand.

"Rock, a couple of sticks of rock. Well, you did ask me," I said.

"I was only joking," he replied.

"I know that Bert but what the heck."

"Thanks," he said. "I'll put them in my locker 'till after work. Can't wait to see the wife chewing on one of these with her false teeth." We both laughed at the idea of it.

"I'm off upstairs," I told him. "Maybe see you later?,"

"Okay son," he said. "Oh, and thanks for the rock, You're okay, Alex."

Now it was time to settle down and get on with the first job the gaffer gave me and I must say what a nice one it was. He asked me to take my time going round the top floor asking who wanted fish and chips bringing in for dinner. Like most people, he and his wife had got a taste for them while on holiday. Apart from that, he had no work for me until after dinner. I offered to help anyone with an extra workload on but the dinner was all he wanted me to do so I got a piece of scrap paper, a pen and wandered around the floor.

This was a dream start to my first day back - dinner collector - and the money all up front as well. The chippy round the corner was in for a real order. Not wanting to be in a long queue, I went off early - first come first served, as they say. The orders were all wrapped up in newspaper and put in three very large brown paper carrier bags for me to carry quickly back to the factory. No time to waste - cold chips were not good for you, my mom always told us. I went round the floor handing out the orders at the speed of light - in those days everyone sat at their work benches. We never had a canteen, some brought their own snap, others had it with a beer or two just around the corner. After dinner, the whole place smelt like just like a fish and chip shop.

The word around the factory was that the move was on just before the end of the month. They were going to move everyone eventually but the different sections would go in order of priority and work space.

Also spreading round the factory floor was the word that Bert, the gaffer downstairs, had been a complete revelation since coming back from the holidays. Everyone had a good word for him. He in turn had a different outlook on life and those who worked under him were much happier, the whole of his floor working like a unit rather than in opposition to each other.

On my way into work on Tuesday morning I turned the corner to find lorries waiting to be loaded up with some very heavy machines which were being transported to the new factory. I still didn't know where it was. The operation went on all day and for most of the week. The word spread like wildfire that the upper floor was to go first. The boss told each of the foremen to notify everyone by handing out a works letter saying when they were to be moved. This they did and, of course, one or two people had a good moan but the dates had been set now. They would either move to the new factory or stop on the ground floor for a while, if there was work for them to do there. Some of the very old hands decided to call it a day.

I had some time to myself on Friday. Nearly all the machines had gone and an easy afternoon was in store so I ambled around the empty floor, looking occasionally out of the grimy windows. Then some great news reached me - we were moving to Aston, the new factory was just of Holborn Hill. Would you believe it? I was going back home.

My last day at the old factory came around and I clocked in for the last time. The ground floor machinery was still silent as the machines had not yet been switched on. I strolled casually towards the stairs leading to the upper floor where I had worked only for a short time, taking my time so as to the feel the emptiness and the lonelyness as all the machines had now gone.

I had no idea how long this old factory had stood here, or how many it would remain. I heard footsteps coming up behind me.

"Morning Alex," a voice called out. "Last day today yeah?" I turned and our gaffer was standing there surveying the area.

We both stood in silence for some time. The next sound I heard was the heavy machines starting up for another day's work on the ground floor. He came closer to me. "Sad really," he said. "So many happy memories of this old place. My wife and I have been here for, now let me think..." He paused and then smiled. "Well, a bloody long time." He took out a handkerchief, blew on it once, then again.

He walked over to some tea chests in the corner and called me to join him. They were full of newspapers and old cardboard, some used rubbing rags and other bits and bobs.

"Alex, take these downstairs would you please. Place them for the miskin-men to take away."

"Yes, leave it all to me. Would you like me to do anything else while I'm here?," I asked.

"No son, no. Just take your time until the lunch siren sounds. I'll be back then."

To kill time, I took the rubbish out of the tea chests then put it back. Then I swept up here and there, hanging it out just about right. I took the last tea chest down and was just about to put it with the other rubbish that had accumulated over the last few days when the siren went.

I ate my corn dog sarnies. The gaffer returned and asked me to help him with some jobs upstairs. There's nothing upstairs, I thought to myself.

"Alex, I'm nipping over to see my wife at the new factory. I'll be an hour or two. Just mess about upstairs and generally keep out of the way," he said with a wink.

I kept myself busy by taking some of the rubbish back upstairs and then bringing it down again, sweeping up the redundant shopfloor in between.

The gaffer returned about four o'clock. We walked up the stairs and took a final look around.

"Go on, hop off home," he said. "See you on Monday, and don't you dare be late." I turned to walk away and had only taken a few steps when he called to me: "Alex." I turned and looked at him. "Thanks son, thanks for your loyalty to me and the work today. Go on, bugger orff."

I turned and casually bunked out of the gate an hour early. He would clock me off, I knew that. He had been good to me from the moment we first met after that incident with Bert and Mr. Cooke.

Come to think of it, I had not seen Bert for a few days. Could he be on holiday, maybe sick.

I heard a whistle from behind me. Should I stop or keep on walking, I thought. Then another whistle came. I had to stop and turn round. Blimey, talk of the Devil. Bert was walking towards me, not in his work clobber, but all dressed up smart.

"Neat suit," I said to him.

"Don't be cheeky," he said with a smile coming across his face. "You scallywag, where are you off to now?"

I was just about to answer his question when he chipped in: "Part time worker, you are." He looked at his watch. "Only ten past four."

"Where have you been?," I asked, changing the subject.

"Oh ermm, had a couple of days off, you know. Well the missus had a few jobs for me to do."

We walked round the corner away out of view just in case anyone was about.

"Are you looking forward to the new factory down Aston?," he asked me.

"Oh yeah. I'm really looking forward to the fresh start. Most people say that its massive and you could get yourself lost in it. Oh yeah, and a brand new canteen."

"Yes, I've nipped in and had a good look round," said Bert. "You're right, its really snazzy. I won't be there for a long time, the ground floor still has work on and the area that I'll be in isn't ready yet.

"Well Alex, you have a nice weekend. Oh, and the wife liked the rock you got. She never bit on it, only licked at it."

We stood laughing for a moment at the very thought of it. Then, he suddenly stopped laughing and a very serious expression came across his face. He held out his hand for me to shake and with fumbling words just said: "Tarrar son."

PUSHING OUR LUCK

"Tea up!," shouted Mom as I walked in the house at the end of another day's work.

"How's your day been?," she asked.

"Okay Mom," I answered. "You been okay too?"

Oh, not bad, may have some good news by Friday night," she told us all.

"Cor Mom, am I getting some extras dosh?," I asked her.

"No you cheeky thing, no extra dosh or anything else if your cheek keeps up."

"I only asked," I said to her with a smile on my face."

"Drop the smile as well," she told me. "No dosh like in don't think you're getting round me as usual."

"Who me Mom?," I asked jokingly.

"Me Mom, me Mom," she answered. "Alex, you don't half try it on."

"I could do with a new overcoat," Dad chipped in.

Mom gave him a right dirty look. "No coat, under or over," she told Dad.

Sheila was just about to add her tuppence worth, opening her mouth to speak, when Mom said: "No, no, no. That's to all three o' yer."

A knock came on the door well after teatime. Dad went to see who it was and then called to me: "Alex, your pals are at the door."

Just as I was about to get up from the chair, in walked Spinner, Nicky and Eamon.

"Listen up Al," Spinner said, "Any plans for this Sunday?"

"Not really given it any thought," I told them.

"We're thinking about Banbury and Oxford," said Spinner.

I shot up the dancers and brought down my timetables and we all sat round the table making our plans. Then Nicky asked: "What's the next shed after Oxford?"

"Didcot," I told him. "Why?"

"Oh no reason, just wondered."

I told them that getting there on a Sunday wasn't a problem, getting into the sheds shouldn't be a problem, the problem would be how much dosh we all had. Silence fell, followed by some umming and ahhing. Everyone was mumbling.

"Look, why don't we all meet back here on Friday after tea and then we can work out how much dosh we have," I said.

Once again our house went silent, the great minds were at work, heads bobbing from side to side as each one of them worked out how much dosh they would have come Friday.

When Friday came we looked at the dosh situation and decided that Oxford would have to suffice. As soon as the lads left, Mom called us all together and asked us to sit down and listen to her news. We all sat, then Mom told us that she was to be the new overall supervisor at Boots the Chemist in town.

Even after that, I never got any extra dosh out of my Mom but she did get me some extra snap for the trip out on Sunday.

Sunday morning - 25th October, 1964 - and Spinner, Eamon, Nicky and me were stood on platform seven at Snow Hill station waiting for the 10 o'clock to Paddington which would take us direct to Oxford.

Just as we got off the train at Oxford, some other spotters told us the shed was really full. Then they said they had just bunked Didcot and Swindon, both were worth doing. With that, they clambered past us and on to the train we were getting off.

For a split second we all looked at each other. No one spoke but we were all thinking the same thing - Didcot and Swindon sounded too good to miss.

We got back on the train, a few more seconds passed, there was a whistle and we were moving out of Oxford station.

We huddled together as we did not want anyone to overhear that we had only had tickets to Oxford. We were a bit worried but it was too late now.

I called the lads to attention. "I've travelled this way many times. Let's just stay together and see what happens. If the guard comes round we'll make up a story. If he doesn't, we'll be getting off at Didcot anyway."

The guard never came round between the two stations. Once that train came to a stand at Didcot we were off and took it easy walking away from the train. I looked casually over my shoulder - no-one looking towards us so I thought we were lucky at that stage but we still had to get back to Oxford later on. I just hoped our luck would hold out.

The train pulled out and we walked towards the booking office. I asked the clerk about the train fare to Swindon. He told me and I returned to tell the lads how much it was. We counted up our cash but we were short.

"Look," I suggested, "we hurry under the subway onto the shed, then as quickly as possible get back to the station and then decide what to do - go back to Oxford or push on to Swindon."

We scurried off towards the shed, in and out very quickly but not before I had taken a photo of Eamon showing off by stopping Standard 4-6-0 73024, and another one in front of Hall class loco 6996 Blackwell Hall.

We then hurried back to the station, arriving just as the Bristol train was announced, stopping at Swindon. The lads, I knew, were not really happy at this situation we were getting into. I asked them who wanted to push our luck to swindon.

"Spinner, what do you say we do?"

He looked at the others, then said: "Yeah, come on - just this once mind you."

128

Nicky looked at me, then Eamon, then glanced at Spinner. "Okay, okay, I'm in," he said.

Eamon said he didn't want to stay on the station alone so we were all heading for Swindon.

On the way I told the lads about an official entrance to the works which also provided access to the shed but by slipping very carefully over the tracks we could avoid detection. Again, the lads were not too pleased with my plan of action. I told them that after coming all this way and risking so much, it would be silly to leave without doing the shed and works.

"There may be a party going round and we might be able to bunk in with them."

Again, no guard checking tickets but also no party going into the works. We left the train, all nice and quiet, and slipped across the track and hid ourselves out of sight in the shed - only 42 locos on. Then we scurried off towards the works, me with my camera hanging round my neck.

We really got a stride on - there was no time to mess about in this place. The works done, it was now time to get out into the cutting up area. With all the numbers down, there was just time for me to get a couple of photos with my Brownie 127all ready. First a quick one of two V2s - 60941 and 60943. Just to the right of them were two Western Region tanks, 8401 and 5257. But surprise of the day was King class loco No. 6000 King George V in the scrapping area, its nameplates and famous bell all removed. The tender was slightly apart from the loco itself.

We were just making a move away from the scrap area when a voice called out to us: "Hey, you lot. Hey there!"

We froze to the spot. A railwayman came towards us. "You'll get lost on your own," he said. Then he pointed further down the long line of dead locos. "Your party's well on it's way out by now. Hurry, or you'll lose them."

I said: "Oh yeah, thanks. Just taking a quick couple of photos. Come on lads, let's catch our party up." I winked at the lads.

Spinner said: "Blimey, they must have missed these locos up here."

Just as we were about to move off, I turned to the railwayman and asked him if all the engines in this area were for scrap.

"Yes, they're all going to be scrapped," he said.

"But this one's King George the Fifth. It isn't going to be scrapped is it?"

"Every engine here is to be scrapped," he insisted.

With that, we grabbed our bags and hurried up to join the none existent party. We really had been lucky that day. Not only did we manage to bunk Didcot shed, and Swindon shed and works, but we never paid any train fare between Oxford and Swindon.

Oxford shed done on the way home and another good day came to an end - all the sheds we did were new to us.

Back home, it was the same mouthwatering routine, Mom putting my dinner in the oven to warm up and me licking my lips in anticipation of what would be on my plate - roast lamb today, Yorkshire puddings, podded peas, carrots and thick, dark brown gravy that had stuck to the edge of the plate and needed a knife to scrape it off. Then a nice cup of tea and my thoughts were already on next week's run.

Actually, my time in the weeks that followed was to be devoted more to home, family and work life with few trips out. A rail strike was the main cause of this inactivity and any trips I did were mainly local.

The next time I got out on a trip of any length was on a wet day in January, 1965. I did Derby, Sheffield, including Tinsley - a new shed for me - and the Staveley sheds.

Derby had a good selection on - 30 steam and 31 diesels - Staveley GC only 24, Barrow Hill 48 and there were 31 diesels on Tinsley.

There wasn't much to look at on the way home from Sheffield to New Street - Millhouses closed, Hasland closed - so I got out some snap and checked my pad to see what, if anything, I had copped. Total number of locos seen was 220, copped 44 altogether - that's those that I could make out - the rain had made the ink run.

As the train headed off towards Birmingham, I sat in a sad frame of mind, my thoughts on all the sheds that were closing now. Hasland, Millhouses, Grimesthorpe, Langwith, Mexy and, in time, Canklow. Jobs were being lost, friends parting company, freight easing off the railway onto road transport, cattle trucks slipping away into history, lines closing, services being axed. The great British Railways we knew and loved was disappearing before our eyes. All I was going to be left with was fond memories of the pleasure these sheds had given me.

The train arrived in New Street. It felt great to be home but thoughts of all the sheds closing were a constant pain deep in my heart. Today I had enjoyed myself - this was Sunday and the date was 3rd January, 1965. I was now entering into my fifth year of train spotting.

I planned my final trip out to Crewe and Stoke for Sunday, 17th January. There was less to see on the way there now - Monument Lane and Wolverhampton Stafford Road sheds had closed though Bushbury and Stafford were hanging on. Crewe was busy enough - 42 on the North shed and 88 on the South shed.

I saw a total of 286 locos but only copped 18. The hobby was now becoming a mad dash to see every steam loco I could before it was too late. I felt a force telling me that my train spotting trips would soon be over - the same force that led me to Aston shed all those years ago.

THE BEST YET

A friend at work said to me: "Alex, the best is yet to come." The best is here, a trip out to beat all trips out - the overnight train from New Street to Glasgow and then the three sheds over in the Edinburgh area.

I managed to get the afternoon, Friday 22nd January, 1965 off work and arrived home at nearly one o'clock. No-one was in so I set to getting all my things together - books, pad, pens, camera, pop, crisps, sweets and two packets of JDs to see me through this long overnight trip. All I had to do now was put my stack of sarnies together. I left a note for Sheila to call me when she got home from school about quarter past four and went off to bed for a couple of hours sleep - not easy to do with all the excitement building up inside me.

I was woken by Sheila's voice from the bottom of the stairs just after four o'clock. Got a good wash down, clean clothes on and went down to help Sis with the teatime arrangements.

"I'll make a nice pot of tea for the folks when they come home," I thought to myself. "Must be extra nice to them - they might give me extra dosh."

The clock ticked away slowly. I was all ready to go and a dark winter's night awaited me outside the front door. A trip into the unknown beckoned - Carlisle was the furthest I had ever been before. What awaited me beyond there I knew not, all the sheds I hoped to bunk would be new ones. I was clockwatching - nine o'clock, nine thirty, nine forty five...

Dad and Uncle Fred came back early from the ale house to take me into town as it was a Friday night and things could be a bit rowdy.

I got my coat on and Mom called me into the kitchen. "Look after yourself," she told me, "and don't trouble with anyone, keep yourself to yourself. Watch what you're up to and keep your wits about you. You're a good lad Alex, enjoy yourself but get yourself home as soon as your trip out's done."

She then gave me a fiver. "Oh, and if there's any change you'd better bring it back to me," she joked. She then gave me a big hug. "See ya, now off with your dad and Uncle Fred."

We all walked over towards the bus stop, Mom standing on the balcony waving us off. The bus came in and we went upstairs, Fred and Dad for a smoke. Me, I just sat there so excited at what the trip held in store.

At New Street I bent my knees and asked the booking clerk for a Child Return to Glasgow. Dad and Fred waited with me for the train to come into platform six. Eventually all the mail and parcels were on and Type 4 diesel No. D331 was ready to go. Dad asked me again if I had got everything.

"Yes, I've checked it a dozen times. I'll be fine Dad. Oh, and thanks for coming to see me off." Then he gave me a fiver, said it was between him and Fred. I told him that Mom had already given me a fiver.

"Oh well, give it me back then," he said. "No son, I'm only pulling your leg."

The platform staff gave the signal, the driver hooted his horn, and with a gentle jerk the train was on its way. I hung out of the carriage window until Dad and Fred were out of sight. As the train went through the tunnel and headed north into the night, I started to feel a bit apprehensive but by the time I reached Wolverhampton the thought of seeing what was on Bushbury shed cheered me up.

The long journey passed reasonably quickly as I kept myself busy trying to make out numbers on the various sheds en-route. The train arrived in Glasgow Central around five thirty. I got off feeling very tired on the one hand and very excited on the other. I checked round the station, wrote down the locos that were there, then tucked my scarf in tight, put on my mom's warm gloves and went off to the first shed in my directory - out at Yoker.

"Hello Glasgae," was the first thought in my head as I looked up towards the sky at 6am on this cold Saturday morning. I had come out of the station and was standing in Hope Street. I asked a newspaper seller the direction to Argyle Street for the bus.

"Turn next right, laddy," he said, pointing out the direction for me. His voice was pure Glasgow and his smile, from one stranger to another, seemed to give the day a good start.

Following the directory to the letter I arrived at the shed area. A diesel shunter was marshalling some wagons together. An old lad came walking over to me. "Morning lad, looking for something?," he asked.

"Yes, the locos on the shed," I replied.

"Oh, I'm sorry, the shed closed some years ago. All the engines have gone, just the shunter working the yard."

My heart and my head dropped. This was not the start I wanted. He could see I was put out by this news.

"Must go, laddy," he said. "Work to do, y'know."

I thanked him, headed away from Yoker and made for the next shed in order of the book.

I informed the clippy on this and every bus that I had never been to Glasgow before, that I was collecting loco numbers and that I would appreciate it if they could put me off at the nearest stop to the shed I wanted. They were really great to me, some never even asked for my fare. On one or two buses, the clippy informed the driver I was in a bit of a rush and I'm sure they found another gear or two.

I was sitting quietly looking out of the window as the bus hurried towards my next shed, 65D Dawsholm, when the clippy came over to me. "Dawsholm steam shed your going to?"

"Yes," I replied

"Och, I'm sure it's closed," said the clippy, going to the front of the bus to ask the driver about it. Other people on the bus felt it was closed too.

The clippy put me off at the stop for the shed and I followed the directory. It was closed alright. Still, no time to dwell on this second disaster, I turned away very quickly. "Must get on," I said to myself. I had to get over to shed number three, 65A Eastfield.

Daylight was breaking through as I returned to Maryhill Road. No bus in sight so I started walking, looking over my shoulder for any approaching bus. Eventually one did come but by then I was fairly close to the shed. Even so, the bus stopped and the clippy beckoned me on board, told me to sit close by as the shed was only a couple of stops away. Another free ride.

I was off and sharply into the shed. "At least this one's open," I thought as my mood improved. "Time for one quick photo." Just enough daylight to snap number 72007 Clan Mackintosh.

This shed done it was now time for a tough one - Cowlairs works. I was in no mood for missing out on any locos now. I followed the book to the works. This quickly bunked, I was on my way to the next one, St. Rollox works and the shed, 65B. I had just left the shed and was walking over a bridge on my way to the next shed, Parkhead, when an A4 Pacific passed slowly underneath with a passenger train. It was No. 60007 Sir Nigel Gresley. I sniffed the steam then rushed to the other side to see it going away - great stuff.

Parkhead shed, 65C, was a treat. Fourteen mixed diesel locos were on - all of them brand spanking new - and just four steam all painted up in different colours. One was green, another yellow ochre, another blue and one brown. Seeing this lot lined up was an impressive sight indeed but I hadn't a clue why they were here. I stood in awe for what seemed like hours then wrote the numbers down in my pad: 49, 103, 123 and 256.

I slipped my rucksack off my shoulders. "Must get a photo or two," I thought. That done, it was back to business and on to the next shed, 65E Kipps. The shed area was only small and just 10 diesels were on but I copped the lot.

Next to get to was 66B Motherwell, a much bigger shed. There were 33 locos on, including a notable Britannia, 70005 John Milton. I'd photographed this loco on banking duty at Perry Bar some time ago.

Next on my list was the large carriage shed just up the bank from Hamilton West station. Just one loco here, a small diesel shunter, D2410. For shunting the carriages, I suppose.

Another bus ride later I was entering the big shed, 66A Polmadie. This was something else. Ninety six locos on, including tanks, Black Fives, two Brits, a few Standards, four A2s and a selection of diesels. I took a photo of one of the A2s, 60512 Steady Aim. My final shed in Glasgow was 67A Corkerhill with 44 on - photographed Standard tank No.80009.

The daylight was starting to fade but I wasn't done yet. Back in the city centre, I made my way over to Queen Street station for the train to Edinburgh and my next shed, 64A St. Margaret's. This was a really dangerous place. Some locos were stabled on my side of the main lines but the shed was on the other side. I wrote down the stabled locos then stood in the dark for nearly half an hour watching an endless procession of trains passing both ways. I stood as close to the track as I could, ready to get across this deadly spot . When eventually a gap came in the traffic, I rushed across into the shed and then waited again for a chance to get back.

Miraculously, I survived this episode and caught a bus back to the city and the next shed at 64B Haymarket, the main shed for Edinburgh to the north and south to Newcastle and London. Just 36 locos were on - Deltics, Peaks, Type 4s, Bo-Bo Type 2s and shunters, not a steam loco in sight.

By now it was dark and cold, and I was feeling hungry and getting tired. I really had to push myself to get to the last shed, 64C Dalry Road. A small shed awaited me and I was soon in and round - just 21 locos on - some shunters, a couple of diesel locos, five Black Fives, four B1s, and a J38.

That was it and I was on the bus through the streets to Waverley station. People everywhere were dressed up and out for a good night on the town. The pubs I passed around eight were well in the groove, people making merry for the moment, music bursting out when the doors opened, then silence again as they closed.

The train got me back to Queen Street just after nine thirty. I had a quick look round and went across to Central. A different man was selling newspapers now. I half heard him shout something about Sir Winston Churchill.

I took a last look up at the sky, glanced around Hope Street and walked onto the station. The Birmingham train was waiting. Once on board I found a warm compartment and set about eating up the rest of my snap. A whistle on the platform, another from the loco and I was going home.

As the train passed Polmadie I stuck my head out of the small sliding window for a last look then closed it, settled back into my seat and shut my eyes.

What seemed like a only few minutes later, I was being poked and prodded as a railwayman's voice penetrated my unconcious state. "Birmingham, Birmingham sonny," said the voice, its owner still shaking me.

Still half asleep, I fumbled for my rucksack, picked up my pen and pad from the small side table, stretched my arms, yawned, scratched my head, placed one foot in front of the other and wished my body to follow my legs. The carriage door was open and, rucksack in hand, I stepped wearily onto platform one. Bag over my shoulders, I dragged my still scrawny little body over towards Union Street. A little more awake now, I climbed aboard the bus and plonked myself down on the nearest seat.

The morning was still pitch black and apart from the bus driver, the clippy and me, no-one else was about. The bus pulled a few yards up to the end of Union Street then turned right past the big stores - Rackhams, Lewis's, Yates's Wine Lodge, The Despatch offices, Steel House Lane cop shop,and the hospital to the left. It turned the corner, passing The Crown pub, the fire station to my right, then I must have closed my eyes for a minute. The clippy gave me a nudge. "Where you getting off son?," he asked.

"Perry Bar," I said.

"Just two more stops then," he advised me.

After more than 30 hours, I was back home. Once inside the house I dumped my bag in the kitchen, hung up my coat, kicked off my boots against the hall wall and dragged my body slowly up the stairs. One by one my clothes hit the floor. I slid slowly into my little bed, pulled the sheets and top cover up and over, nearly smothering my face. Then my eyes, heavy from lack of sleep, closed and I was gone.

Altogether I had seen 468 locos. It was an all-time record for me - if I'd been able to travel there and back in daylight it might have been as many as 600. The number of steam locos just exceeded the diesels - 238 steam and 230 diesel - while I copped 156 steam locos and 175 diesels. This trip was never to be surpassed.

Just one reason why the Scotland trip would never be bettered - A4 Pacific No. 60031 *Golden Plover* stands by the wooden coaling stage at 65B, Glasgow St. Rollox shed.

A BRUSH WITH THE LAW

Monday, 25th January, 1965 - I'll never forget this day. I'll remember it for as long as I live with heartache, anger and a variety of other emotions.

I had just one shot left to finish off my Scotland film so after work on Monday I decided to bunk Aston shed and use it on whatever was there. It was while I was trying to climb the brick wall on Holborn Hill that disaster struck.

As I pulled myself up, my Brownie 127 crashed to the floor, knocking a hole in the side and ruining the entire film, and all my wonderful Scottish pictures with it.

I had no stomach for my next trip to Eastleigh and Southampton Docks but, geed up by the folks at home, I picked myself up and off I went.

"You'll only mope about the house all day if you don't go," said Mom.

On the way back while bunking Banbury shed I met a lad who told me about a coach trip from Birmingham to sheds in the South West in about three weeks time.

I was reasonably pleased with Eastleigh and Southampton. I'd obviously liked a few more cops than the 46 I managed but I did have a nice time and another trip to Cardiff this Sunday, 7th February, 1965, was already on paper.

Canton, my first shed of the day, was utterly packed out with all sorts of diesel locos. Everywhere I turned, so stood a diesel. I raced round like a nutter, my pen and pad working furiously. Next was Cardiff East Dock still with plenty of steam locos on. From there I headed back to the city centre and a local train to a new shed I was about to bunk, 88C Barry along with the works and yard - but I was in for a real shock. The train approached Barry station and into view came a sight that I was not prepared for - rows and rows of dead steam locos filled the yard on the works side of the shed.

I did the shed first then, not really wanting to go any further, I stopped and just looked on these locos with such a sad feeling in my heart. Tears started to trickle down my face, my pen and pad were put away in my pocket as I just stood there looking at them. I could hear them crying out to me, like someone lying in hospital dying very very slowly.

There was no dignity here, not in just standing about with rags tied over their chimneys. Some were rusting away, others had parts taken off or stolen, messages - some rude - were chalked all over their bodies, cab windows were smashed, coupling rods missing, once proud names gone. I didn't usually notice the cold on my trips out in winter but right now I felt chilled to the marrow.

I heard footsteps on the ballast coming up behind me, it was a couple of loco spotters.

"Hello," they said in what seemed like London accents.

"Bleedin' shame," one lad said to me.

"Yeah, a real sad sight to see," I said.

"Got 'em all?," the other lad asked.

"No, I don't really want to write the numbers down." They could see I was really saddened by this sight.

"Look mate," one lad said, "you might look back one day on this trip, just like we might, and you'll have no record to show what was here today. Come on, walk round wiv us."

I did but without much enthusiasm. This was the moment when it hit me that steam was really coming quickly to an end and time was running out.

We took our time walking round the cemetery. Most of the locos were tanks - 2-8-0s, 0-6-0s, 0-6-2s and 2-6-2s. There were some Hall class locos, a single Jubilee, two Kings and a good few Southern locos - S15s, Ns, a few Battle of Britain, West Country and Merchant Navy Pacifics.

Another week passed and the sadness of Barry faded. This coming Friday I was to undertake the toughest and longest trip I had ever been on. This all hinged on the information given to me by the lad I had bumped into at Banbury a couple of weeks ago. The trip was to the South West but which sheds I didn't know. The coach left town at midnight on Saturday night but before that I was doing a trip on Friday night, a very cold and dull evening, 19th February, 1965.

I advised the folks that I was off to York, then Darlington and all the sheds in the Wakefield area. I'd then return as soon as possible for a short break and to freshen up. I asked Mom to get some extra snap in for me - a few bottles of pop, two extra packets of JDs - and to make up some more sandwiches. She asked why I wanted the extra. I told her that as soon as I got home I would have some tea, a change of clothes and then try to get on the Saturday midnight trip to the South West.

Mom and Dad just looked at me and for a while never said a word. Eventually Dad asked: "How are you getting on this South West trip at midnight?"

I told him and Mom that it was an organised coach trip.

"Oh well, that's different," said Mom. She then asked me the coach firm.

"To be honest with you, I only have a little bit of information from a lad I bumped into at Banbury shed." I told Mom and Dad that I would earn some extra dosh and pay extra for my keep.

"We're not worried about that, Alex," Mom said. "That Scotland trip knocked you about a bit and that was only a few weeks ago. Don't you think it's a bit soon for another big trip?"

137

She was right but I explained that this was just a one off and I really did not want to miss the chance.

"What if the coach is fully booked?," she asked.

"Mom, I promise I'll get myself straight home and go somewhere else on Sunday," I said.

They looked at each other again then Mom said: "You're a good lad, Alex, and you've never brought any trouble home. Go on son, but take care eh."

The train from New Street pulled into York at about a quarter to midnight. Directory in hand, I was going to bunk one of the great sheds, 50A.

So far so good. Walking up and down the lines of locos in the long yard, I could hear a voice shouting something over the yard tannoy system Three or four times I heard the same sound but I couldn't make out any of the words. I was between the last two lines of locos when I noticed a distant light coming towards me. I joked to myself that it was very nice of somebody to shine a light on the numbers for me. Not funny - a railwayman had been sent out by the shed foreman to get me and take me to him in his office. This was not to be taken lightly.

The foreman sat at his desk, a blue dustcoat covered up his massive frame. He turned to me as I stood there waiting.

"I've been .... calling you, you little .... for the last ten or more minutes. I've more important things to do than mess about with this microphone. No permit, no pass I bet. You just roll up, roll in, then roll out as if nothing else in the world matters, right? Am I right?"

I was just about to say sorry when he launched into another blistering attack on me, a fine volume of words coming out of his mouth. "Now you're going to say sorry and it won't happen again, yes? Yes, I'm right again, aren't I."

The railwayman that had brought me out of the yard turned and went outside.

"Sit down there," the foreman told me pointing to a chair. He reached for an old silver looking teapot and poured a cup of tea for himself, looked over at me and poured out another cup. He then opened a tin and took out a couple of sandwiches and four dainty little fairy cakes which he lined up neatly on the desk. I was trying very hard not to smile - here was this really big, big foreman about to eat fairy cakes. He passed me a sandwich then gave me two of his cakes. We sat there together and never spoke. The tea drunk, sandwich eaten, fairy cakes gone down a treat, he wiped his hands on a cloth, turned to me and told me to .... off.

I crossed the track running parallel to the lines that ran alongside the shed, not far from the little works that I did manage to bunk.

I arrived in Darlington around two am. At the barrier a young police constable was in conversation with the ticket snapper. He looked at me as the snapper asked for my ticket but didn't speak. I felt in my coat pocket, keeping the shed directory in my hand out of sight of both the snapper and the officer. I felt sure that the officer would follow me.

I was just about to turn under the railway bridge when a voice called out to me: "Excuse me, excuse me." I knew it was the policeman. I stopped, he came closer to me. "Where you off to at this hour?," he asked.

"I'm off to the shed just around the corner."

"Got a permit?," he then asked me.

"No, I've never had one," I told him.

"What do you mean you've never had one?"

"Well, I mean I've never had one," I told him again.

There was silence for a moment, then he asked me my name, age and address. I gave him all the details and, thinking of Melvin, spoke really nice and friendly to him.

"Right," he said in a friendly manner, "you just come with me."

He had spoken to me all the time in a friendly way but he now seemed a little more at ease himself.

"Train spotting are you?," he asked me.

"Yes, I've never been to this shed before," I said as I walked with him to wherever he was taking me. We swung left into Yarm Road then into Green Street and it was then that I knew we were heading towards the shed. He sort of marched me into the foreman's office, then set about explaining what he and I were doing there. To my complete astonishment, the foreman told the officer that seeing as he had brought me to the shed he should be the one to take me round. The officer was really taken aback.

The policeman and I left the foreman's office. We stood for a while surveying all the locos that were about the shed area. He made no move to go or anything. The worst that could happen now was that we could go straight back to the station, the best thing for us to do, in my opinion, was to bunk the shed. Then again, I would think that. Then he came out with a real gem. He asked me just how long it would take us to get round this depot.

"If I follow you, about half an hour but if you follow me we'll be in and out of this shed and back to the station in less than that," I explained.

He looked at me then said: "That fast are you?"

"No," I said, "faster."

For the first time, he managed to raise a smile. "Are you telling me you're that fast?"

"Oh yes, I'm really that fast."

He pulled up his tunic sleeve, looked at his watch. The time, he told me, was just coming up to 2.30am. "You're telling me we can be back at the station before three?"

"If we stand here any longer it just might be after that," I said, smiling.

139

"Well," he said looking about the place, "let's go."

He followed me all around the shed, up and down the rows of locos, some dead, some in steam. The shed bunked, we were just about to find the side door into the old workshops when he came out with another question on train spotting. He asked me if I would have still tried to do the shed if he had taken me back to the station. I said that I would not have gone home without doing this shed. He knew I was serious.

The workshops bunked, we were now on our way back to the station. Just walking up the ramp, he stopped and said: "You're a very fearless person aren't you."

"Yes I am," I answered. "Two years ago the shed foreman at Banbury called me and my two friends fearless ghosts. We would roll up, roll in and roll out without anyone knowing we'd ever been there - the fearless ghosts we were."

He smiled and we walked on. He took me to the waiting room - a glowing fire on the go - then offered me his hand to shake. This I did. Then he revealed that was the one and only time he had ever walked round a steam shed. He also owned up that, between him and me, he'd really enjoyed it.

"Get your head down," he told me. "I'll tell the platform staff not to trouble you but to wake you up just before they go off duty at 06.00 hours." He walked towards the waiting room door, stopped for a second, turned and looked at me. "Goodbye fearless ghost," he said. A smile came across his face, the door opened and he walked out onto the platform.

I was the only person in the waiting room. I laid my rucksack on the long seat and curled up for some much needed sleep. The bench was hard, I tossed and turned for most of the night, changing to this position then another but I did manage to get a couple of hours kip.

An old lad came into the waiting room. "Hello," he said. "It's nearly quarter to six." In his hand was a chipped cup with tea in it.

"Oh, thanks," I said. He walked out and I got myself together for the first train out which was just after six. I grabbed a sandwich then dipped a couple of JDs in the very welcome tea. The cup of tea was just the ticket and by now I was feeling great with another day before me.

I returned the chipped cup to the staff room and boarded my train to Leeds. Once in Leeds I went off to find the train to Bradford - I had all the times written down on a piece of paper. The first shed to bunk was 56G Hammerton Street where there were just eight diesel shunters on with all the DMUs. Low Moor, 56F, was next to bunk - just 14 steam locos on here, then Manningham - only eight steam locos plus four diesel shunters. Neville Hill had just 14 steam locos on plus six diesels. Wakefield, 56A, was the largest shed so far, 87 locos on - 72 of them steam.

I arrived back in New Street around half four, the bus home was packed with Saturday shoppers. Once home I had some scoff and a couple of hours' kip in the chair. My mom, God bless her, had made my sandwiches for the South West trip and served a hot dinner up at seven thirty. I cleaned out and repacked my rucksack then tried to calm myself down a bit before heading off into town at 11 o'clock.

It was about 11.25 when I arrived in town. The rain was pouring down so I did a quick whiz round New Street station, as much for shelter from the wind and rain as anything else.

The coach was parked in Station Street, just down the steps from New Street. A few people were already in their seats and as time ticked by more and more of them arrived and got on the coach. The rain was still pouring down as I stood there watching the coach fill up. I was very tired, lonely and cold, and just wanted to go back home to bed. Even if this trip was all booked up I'd still had a great trip out to Yorkshire and Darlington.

The time was approaching midnight. The club secretary stepped down off the coach, looked at his watch, looked at me all wet, then stepped back on the coach. The engine started up and the doors closed in front of me. Then, with a wooshing sound they opened again. The secretary came off the coach, looked at his watch then glanced in my direction. I was standing only a matter of yards from the coach doors. He took another look at me then, looking up and down Station Street, asked if I had booked with his party. I said that I was only told about the trip by a fellow spotter and that I was only there on spec, but if there was a seat, I'd be grateful.

"That's it," he said, "time we were going." He told me to get on the coach and told the driver that he was ready to leave.

"It's four pounds, is that okay?," he asked me.

"Yes, sure," I said.

"Find a seat for yourself."

I was glad to get on board out of the rain, also glad to find a seat next to a lad who was asleep. I fumbled for the four quid and gave it to the secretary.

"Look." he said, "I'll be back in a moment, just need a word with the driver. Oh, and I'll bring you an itinery, also details of next week's trip."

He swayed from side to side as the coach picked up speed out of the city. A minute or two later I could see him swaying again as he headed back towards me.

"Right now," he said. "This is the one we are on." He passed me a small piece of paper then another piece of paper. "This is the one for next week." I glanced at the one we were on first. He then asked if I'd been to any of the sheds on the list.

"Errmm, yes. I've done Eastleigh, Southampton Docks and Bath Green Park. The others are all new to me." This pleased us both, six new sheds.

"I'll see you at Salisbury," he said and went to his seat.

The lad next to me fidgeted for a second as I got myself sorted out. Now lovely and warm. I thought to myself: "Just right, now for some kip."

A jolt from the coach woke most of us up. Some lads were already awake. Then there was another jolt.

"Sorry lads," came this voice from the front. "It's this bloody fog, can't see my hand in front of my face." The fog was really bad, the lad next to me pressed his nose up to the window and said he couldn't see a thing.

Just then the driver stopped the engines, the doors opened and he got out. A few moments later he revealed that we were as close to the shed as he could get us. We had arrived in a thick blanket of fog at 70E Salisbury. The secretary told us to hang on for a while.

He and the driver went missing for about five minutes then returned out of the fog. "Right lads, we're okay for the shed," the secretary announced. One by one we piled off the coach, filed round the shed and then marched back onto the coach.

The time was now coming up to 4am. Couldn't see anything but fog. After a double check that everyone was back on board, the driver eased his way out of the shed area and we were Eastleigh bound.

It was about 6am when we pulled up just short of the bridge over to the works and shed. For the second time, the secretary disappeared into an office block.

He returned with a big smile on his face then told us to stay close by and watch out for the third rail that ran near to where the locos were. Once again we followed him pied piper style, writing down the numbers and bumping into each other when a lad in front stopped without warning.

It was just after seven when we were all back on the coach which was really buzzing with the excitement of doing Eastleigh. Off we went to the next shed, Southampton Docks. I would have loved to have heard what the secretary told the gateman at the docks entrance but we got in, on foot. I was convinced that he never had a permit for any of the sheds we went to.

The sun was trying its best to break through as we got back onto the coach after Bournemouth shed. I was feeling hungry by now, time for some scoff. The lad next to me had his head buried in his pad. We hardly said two words all the way through the trip, just "great shed" or "copped a few on this shed." There were one or two noisy lads on board but they were some way away from me. This lad, being quiet, suited me as I was tired after having been all the way to Darlington and back the night before.

The weather, believe it or not, was really hot and sunny when we arrived at Weymouth. After bunking the shed we even went down to the beach for a while. Some of the lads chipped in and bought a plastic football. We got teams up and had a great kick-about in our bare feet. The secretary and the driver had somehow managed to wangle two fancy coloured deckchairs. The hour on the beach passed quickly and we were soon climbing back on the coach, bringing half the beach with us. There was sand between our toes, up our legs, in our trouser turnups and in our hair from heading the ball.

We were now heading back towards Birmingham and the next shed on the itinery was 83E Yeovil, a small shed with just 12 locos on. We were in and out in no time and off to the next one, 83G Templecombe, just 15, all steam except for a single Western class diesel, D1032. The next shed was a bit larger, 83C Westbury and it had a decent sized yard but just 20 locos on, four of them shunters, plus a couple of tanks, two Halls and three Hymeks. The final shed was Bath Green Park, 18 on but every one steam. Now that's a nice way to finish a really good trip.

With the daylight fading and another cold winters night looming we headed back for home. Two inches of snow had fallen in Birmingham while I had been away so in 24 hours I'd seen four different kinds of weather. - wind and rain in Birmingham, dense fog in Salisbury, warm sunshine in Weymouth and snow back in Birmingham.

The secretary came round with a clipboard, taking names and giving out information for next weekend's trip to the North West. The fare was just £3 and I put my name down to reserve a seat. So did the lad next to me.

The North West trip was to be my last big trip out and the locos seen were to be some of the final entries in my last pad. We did a total of 12 sheds around Lancashire and Manchester and saw 467 locos, of which I copped 105. It had been another great trip but I never went with the club again.

Just four more entries went in my pad. The first was a trip to Tywyn for some unknown reason, saw 55 locos on the way there and back, copped only 11. The next trip, on 24th July, 1965, was again to Tywyn. This time I saw 48, copped only six. The last but one entry I remember as if it were yesterday. I'd met a girl in Tywyn, we exchanged addresses and I promised to visit her for the day. On the journey I saw just 24 and copped - three.

My last trip was to Crewe. Just 28 locos on Crewe North, mostly diesels, and some electrics near the station. Steam locos included two Brits and a couple of 9Fs. There were 71 locos over at Crewe South, a good and interesting variety but I copped only four of them. Just seven locos were on the little shed at Gresty Lane but I did cop a tank loco, 6665.

My final day's train spotting had come to a sad end with just 14 cops to show for it. I stood a few yards from Gresty Lane shed thinking of the days when I visited these places with Melvin and David, very happy and cutting memories, running round the sheds and yards, the turntables I had been privelaged to stand on, the fantastic shed foremen.

I made my way back to Crewe station. It was very quiet today, not many lads about collecting loco numbers. Times were changing alright.

A BAD MOVE

The weeks and months flew by into 1966. With Christmas and New Year over, all of us, including my sister, were now at work.

Mom had switched jobs and was now a supervisor at the old people's home just a minute's walk from our house. Sheila was working at the Birchfield Road library - a stone's throw from her old school and the house - Dad had a very well paid little number just 15 minutes away on the bus and me, I was doing okay for myself, just a two stop train ride from the factory in Aston.

We were all living very well and enjoying the good life. The house was all decorated in the latest fashion, furniture all brand spanking new and every-thing in the household was great. Money was plentiful though we never, under any circumstances, mentioned it outside our four walls.

But things were to change.

When we lived in the old back to backs in Aston, my mom had a friend called Floss. Like us, Floss and her husband Ted moved out of Aston - only they went to Weymouth, in Dorset.

They stayed in touch through letters and phone calls, and during summer, 1965, Floss invited my mom and dad to stay with them for a weekend.

They took Sheila with them, travelling down on the Friday and returning late Sunday evening. I stayed at home and hung around the house.

They came back full of praise for Floss and Ted and for the break they had laid on. My mom was really pleased with the weekend and Dad was very impressed with what he had seen. The weather had been good too - it's amazing how a little sunshine can make things look so much better.

We went on living the good life but some time after the Weymouth trip my mom was making overtures to the housing department in Broad Street about a house exchange.

Unknown to me at the time, they were looking for a move to Weymouth. Ted worked at Cavendish's brewery and reckoned to have a job lined up for my dad; Floss also had a job organised for my mom. On the strength of this my folks were planning a move to Weymouth later in the year.

Midway into January, Mom received notification from the housing depart-ment that an exchange was on the cards. A family from Weymouth were looking to get back to Birmingham and wanted to visit our house and the surrounding area.

They came and liked what they saw. Our family, with the exception of myself, visited their home in Weymouth. They too liked what they saw and the exchange was set in motion.

This was late January. I asked my folks if they were sure about the move. I also asked if they were a hundred per cent certain that the jobs Floss and

Ted had lined up for them were still on. I urged them to get in touch with Floss and get details about the job at the brewery.

For some reason I smelt a rat. The people who visited us wanted to get back to Birmingham just a little too much. They were very pushy.

I kept on at my mom, then switched my attentions to Dad. I was almost at the begging stage when they became very intolerant of my continuing attitude towards the move.

By early February, Mom, Dad and me were still at loggerheads over this Weymouth business - it wasn't like them not to check out all the details. I learned from them as a little lad down in Aston to make sure of all the facts and try to get to the bottom of all that's important in life. They just seemed unmoved by all my requests concerning this move to Dorset.

"Good news," they told us after we had had our tea.

Mom and Dad said they had contacted Floss and Ted as we were all very concerned about the eventual move from Birmingham and asked them for assurances about the jobs.

Floss wrote back to Mom stating that everything was as planned. I asked to see the letter but Mom refused to show me it, saying I was over concerned. I asked Dad if he had seen the letter; he told me that Mom knew what she was doing and that the move would be a good one for all of us.

He had never seen the letter. For the first time in my life I did not believe my mom. A nagging feeling deep down inside me kept returning with the same thought - a rat!

I handed in my two weeks notice at the factory on Monday 14th February, 1966 and asked Mr. Cooke to keep the matter private. I picked up all the money due to me on the Friday then went to say goodbye to Mr. Cooke and to the gaffer and his charming wife. He shook me by the hand and wished me well, his wife looked upset by the farewell. Anyway, I needed to make a clean break, it was time to get out and away.

To pack that job in, I think, was the biggest mistake I ever made. From that moment, I believe I went down hill all the way.

As usual, when I got home I gave my unopened pay packet to my mom and she,as usual, opened it and gave me so much. On this particular Friday, I asked for a small loan of a few extra quid as I wanted to get myself some new gear. She gave me £5.

I told her nothing about the job - or the lack of one, nor did I mention that I was about to pack a small holdall and leave home the next morning. I had nothing planned apart from waiting for them both to leave for work. I would then have a large breakfast to keep me going, pack what clobber I thought I would need and as much snap as I could carry.

My clobber all packed, I went upstairs and woke Sheila. After she had come round, I told her I was leaving home because I felt this business to do with Weymouth was a big mistake and I felt that in the long run it would cost us dearly. Sheila was a good kid, she understood my motives. She gave me a kiss and then told me to look after myself. She said she would say nothing to the folks about my leaving unless asked.

I caught a train from New Street to Nottingham and collected locos en-route. Later that afternoon I bunked Nottingham Midland shed, then spent a few hours just walking around, thinking to myself.

I came across a sign indicating the road to Manchester and got a lift in a van to Piccadilly station. I wrote down all the numbers there and then bunked a train to Crewe.

It was dark when I arrived and I had to spend the night in a real rough doss house. I hardly slept a wink for the fighting that went on until late in the night - I kept my clothes on, my money down my socks and slept with my shoes under the pillow. About eight the next morning someone knocked on the door calling me for breakfast.

I was glad to be alive, let alone awake. I washed then hurried down the stairs for some breakfast.

The lady who ran this joint was okay to me, she could tell I was a bit scared by all that had happened the previous night. She asked in a friendly manner where I was off to next. I felt sure she knew I was on the move.

I answered her by saying: "Oh, just up north, er Carlisle way."

I was the only one up at that time. She made sure no-one else was about then gave me some extra bacon, another egg and a rather large sausage. She smiled and said: "Half that lot won't be eating this morning. They've had too much beer in their bellies."

I thanked her and began to really tuck in, washing the lot down with two mugs of tea. She was really good to me and I could tell she hated this dive.

My bag rested on the floor between my legs as the final drop of tea went down. When I asked her if I could carry the plates back to the kitchen for her, she gave me a bright smile that I bet was hardly ever seen by the bunch who lived there.

She looked so lovely in her different coloured pinny, a bit of make up and lipstick and a star would come forth. So bright yet such hidden beauty. I was only 17 and a bit, she was in the thirties I guess.

She took the plates from my hand and by true accident our finger tips touched very softly, so gently I just wanted to fall into her arms. I was a 17 year-old kid and I had no idea what I was doing here.

I grabbed my bag and, slowly looking in her direction, opened the lodging house door. Oh God, I wish I'd never left her. The door closed behind me and I felt a heaviness in my heart, probably due to falling in love for the first time. For a few seconds I stood on the doorstep, staring down at the blood-stains from last night's brawling and thinking whether I should go back in or walk away.

I chose to walk on but I had only gone a couple of yards when I heard the door. I turned quickly and there she stood holding a pint of milk.

"Quick," she said. "Put this into your bag, you might get thirsty on your journey."

I took it from her slowly and as I did she edged her way towards me and gave me a small kiss. Then she hurried back into the house. I watched her every step before turning away. A feeling of total unhappiness ran amok inside me. I wanted to go back more than anything in the world but things were not clear - she was probably twice my age, she could be married. I thought up all sorts of reasons why I should not go back.

The time was just around nine o'clock. I got a lift in a van to the M6, another van to a junction somewhere, then a car to Wigan Springs Branch shed. I bunked the shed in nice warm sunshine - 80 on - then sat near the entrance thinking out my next move.

I returned to Wigan station, bunked the train to Preston, then bunked another to Lancaster. I paid 5/6 to Workington, bunked the shed there, just 24 on, a nice mixture though.

Then I thumbed a lift to a place called Wigton and from there got a ride in a car to Carlisle very, very late on Sunday and bunked Kingmoor shed in the early hours of Monday morning. I then went on to Upperby shed - 24 mixed locos on.

When I got back to the station, I noticed a lad hovvering around the hotel nextdoor. I explained my position to him. He was great - brought me some sandwiches, a mug of hot tea and a plate of biscuits then told me to get my head down inside for an hour or two. He said he would give me a shout about 5.30 because the other night porter came on duty at five to six.

I didn't wake up until the lad shook me and told me that it was coming up to 5.45. He said he had forgotten all about me as he himself had been having an hour in the chair. He rushed off and came back with a drop of coffee. It was a bit cold but I thanked him and drank it all up.

I got my gear together and walked out of the hotel into a cold Monday morning. I got a lift in a lorry to Barrow-in-Furness Loco, arrived in daylight and bunked the place - 24 on. A funny load of locos - a Brit., tanks, Jinties, a couple of Black Fives, some shunters, a Bo-Bo diesel and five Metropolitan Vickers Co-Bos.

That shed done, I thumbed a ride to Carnforth, it was nearly dinner time when I got in. I scurried round the shed - another good cross section of locos on.

My next move was a very long journey by cars, van and a long distance lorry to Bristol. I did the shed shortly after being dropped off a mile or so from the station. There were 25 diesels on, including D0280 Falcon. Next I got a variety of lifts to Taunton. Did the shed, not many on, just 17, then spent the night sleeping rough in an old unused part of the shed, a few none too clean rags to keep me warm.

The next day saw me travel down to Weymouth, again by a varied assortment of road transport arriving very late that evening. I headed to Floss and Ted's house hoping for a rest.

On the way I stopped off at a rather large restaurant to get a few cakes and a cup of tea, and have a swill down to tidy myself up.

I didn't want them to know why I was in Weymouth apart from looking them up. They made me very welcome though they did ask me a few questions. I had a great night's sleep and woke up to a sunny day, 2nd March, 1966. They left me some breakfast with a note saying they would be back home at 5pm. I spent the day loooking around the town, bunking the shed - 16 on - and sunning myself on the beach.

I stayed with Floss and Ted until Saturday morning when I left after breakfast. At that point I had been away from home exactly one week.

Weymouth seemed okay, the weather was nice and the place was clean and tidy - it might be the right move to make after all. Floss and Ted seemed alright, but this nagging doubt would not let up.

It was eleven o'clock when I got to Westbury. Only four locos were on the shed area - a shunter, a Hymek, a BR Standard and a West Country, 34033 Chard. From there I got a lift to Bath, bunked Green Park - 19 locos on - then to Bristol Bath Road for the second time in a week. There were 40 diesels on, ranging from Peaks and Hymeks to Warships, Westerns, 47s and 37s.

It was about teatime so I had a bit to eat on the station and stuffed the odd sandwich into my pocket. My next move was to get out of the city and head off somewhere.

I arrived back in Birmingham about 10pm and stood looking up at my front door. I looked long and hard, thinking about whether or not to go up and try to explain how I felt about all that had led up to my leaving home for a week. I felt I couldn't do this so I turned away and walked to Uncle Fred's house down in Aston - taking my time because it was Saturday night and he would be out with Dad down the dogs or the Crown and Cushion.

Fred arrived at the top of the grove close on midnight. He approached me and not to alarm him I called out that it was me.

"Alex, Alex," he shouted. "What the bloody hell are you doing here? I've just left your mom and dad and they're worried sick about you."

We walked down the grove into Fred's house and sat up till nearly two o'clock just trying to understand why I had done what I had done. Fred was really great to me, he always had been, and was clever enough to take it all in and help with the situation that had caused my folks so much worry. I explained all the reasons for leaving home and how I had been to Weymouth to look it over for myself, and how I felt so much better in myself for doing it.

I stayed with Fred that Saturday night, also Sunday and Monday nights. On Tuesday morning my mom was at Fred's house to meet me. I was glad to see her, we both landed up crying in each other's arms.

Fred left for work leaving Mom and me to sit and talk the situation over. He gave Mom the key and asked her to lock up when we left. We sat talking about all that I had been up to though she was careful in asking about Weymouth or Floss and Ted, and she never mentioned the jobs they said they had arranged.

We finished talking about 9.15 and Mom said we should get off home. I agreed but just then, thinking about home, told Mom to carry on, I would catch up with her in a short while.

I needed to be alone with my thoughts so what better place to be in than Aston shed. I lifted myself up to look over the high wall, there were a few on but I only stayed a couple of minutes and continued to Saltley. Bunked the shed the for the last time - 44 locos on. The line of Scots had gone, Brush diesels were scattered all round this massive shed, the three turntables and the locos that turned on them would soon be just a memory.

I could hear Melvin's voice telling me to run here, go there. For a moment I thought I saw David whizzing round the shed, his blonde hair flopping across his bright sparkling face, and Melvin's large frame moving calmly about the shed - for a big lad he did move very gracefully, and he was fast off the mark. Needed to be at times.

I felt myself reaching out and for a second I tried to touch them, but they were only a mirage, only there in my mind. I felt great sadness, I knew my spotting days had ended where they started.

I put my pad and pen away inside my coat pocket and slowly walked down the slope, turning for one last look. I sniffled and the tears began to trickle down my face. My coat sleeve was once again on nose and eye wiping duty. But these tears were not to be absorbed. Still they rolled from my eyes, down my neck, onto my shirt, falling like raindrops onto the concrete.

I walked the streets for the best part of March, 1966. I was looking for a job every single day, up early and never coming home till teatime. The days of being able to walk in and out of jobs willy nilly were close to an end. The last Friday in March I got myself hired as a lorry driver's mate working at a big warehouse in Witton.

The weekend flew by and I was outside the main gate just as a few of the others were arriving, the time about five to seven. A chap arrived with some keys and I let everyone else go in first.

I casually eased my way into an area where a large lorry filled the entrance. A chap came walking towards me.

"Morning," he said. "You're the new lad eh?"

"Yes, my first day," I answered.

"You come with me," he said as he began showing me round this massive place.

"Big 'un, in't it," he said to me.

"Cor, big ain't the word," I said.

"Now then, this goes here, that there, over there that should go. Right, now over here we have these and those go into there...."

My head was spinning already with him twisting and turning, showing me where everything was to go, or in some cases not to go, but after an hour or so I had caught the drift of what was required of me.

"Oh, and that's the lorry," he said.

I noticed about half a dozen other chaps around the warehouse, some packing the lorry, others moving large shipments of food about the place. A little truck dashed between the stacks of food.

"That's the Scanner truck driver. Just a tip," he winked, "keep out of the way, he thinks he's in a race all the time, bit of a lunatic at times." He started laughing then said: "Have to be to work in this joint all these years."

It was just coming up to 4.45pm when the lorry driver came up to me. He stopped, then looking me up and down for a while, asked if I was his new mate. I was about to answer when he told me: "Get in the truck." His manner was a bit on the rough side so into the front of the truck I jumped.

"Keep yer mouth shut, can yer?," he asked me.

I never said a word.

"Keep yer mouth shut?, I asked yer," he repeated.

Again, I said not a word.

"Oi, I'm talking to you," he said looking over at me. "Deaf are yer?"

Still I didn't speak and by now he was getting really ratty. The lorry pulled out of the warehouse and he never spoke again until he asked where I lived. I gave him my address. Then he said: "You heard me ask that, dent yer?"

I was now angry and he was getting more and more angry with my silence. He was about to make a speach when I interrupted him: "Look mate," I said, "You asked me if I could keep my mouth shut, yeah?"

He was about to say something, his mouth hung open and I blocked his words again: "By me not answering you that was a sign that I could keep my mouth shut."

He hit the brakes and pulled the lorry over to the kerb. "Listen, you wanna earn some big money?"

I thought to continue playing him on. "How big's this money?," I asked. He fidgeted then from his back pocket produced what I guessed was around £500. I never moved a muscle, just looked, then snorted: "That's big money?"

He went crackers, banging his hands on the steering wheel and bouncing about in his seat. I just sat there taking no notice of him. I half opened the passenger door then, looking across at him, said: "I'll walk the rest of the way home, thanks mate."

I jumped down, closing the door after me. He opened his door and came at me like a bull. He was about three yards away when I burst out laughing. He stopped dead in his tracks, must have seen the funny side of his tantrums and joined me on the pavement, laughing.

"I like you," he told me.

"Oh, that's nice. I don't like you at all," I said. We carried on laughing our heads off.

The week went by and I picked up my first paypacket - £7, 11 shillings and sixpence. The lorry driver gave my mom £40. As the weeks passed her food bill came down to nearly zero. We had never seen so much good food on the table - and each Friday the driver gave Mom £40.

We travelled all around Birmingham delivering food supplies, shop after shop after shop. Money seemed no problem to this fella or to the others I became aquainted with. They were all really great to me and we had some laughs, especially telling the story about when my driver asked if I could keep my mouth shut.

It was too good to last. The exchange that Mom had been trying to arrange over the months had finally come through. It was very strange but on the same day that Mom advised me of the moving date, I was arriving back from being out on the rounds when a fella in the warehouse pulled me over to one side and told me to get out. I was to hand in my week's notice.

The gaffer accepted my notice without question - the whole set up had been tumbled. On my last day, the driver took me home early. We stopped just before the spot where he usually dropped me off.

"Alex, take this." He handed me £250. "I trust you with it," he said. "You're not a rat. Now get yourself off home."

I opened the lorry door, stepped down, closed the door and he pulled away. It would be many years before I met up with him again. I kept the money tight inside my back pocket.

A large lorry was parked outside the maisonnettes - we were finally moving from Perry Bar to Weymouth. The house was in uproar, everything everywhere, what a mess.

The removals van was eventually loaded up. Mom sat at the front, Dad, Sheila and myself in the back on the sofa. The lorry stopped now and then just to give us some fresh air.

We arrived in Weymouth late on Friday evening, everyone helped with the furniture. When the lorry was unloaded the two lads were asked if they wanted to stay the night. The gaffer said they had a chitty for a hotel and would we vouch for them staying there as they wanted to get home and still collect the bed and breakfast money.

We spent the weekend sorting out our new home and by Sunday we were looking something like. The rooms were arranged, the kitchen larger than the old house, the living room bigger too, and there was a front and rear garden. I have to say the whole house was tops. The neighbours either side of us were very friendly and helpful too.

On Tuesday Floss and Ted came over to welcome us to Weymouth. Mom and Dad chatted to them for hours while Sheila and I looked round the area. We were unprepared for the bad news that greeted us when we got back.

The job at the brewery which Ted had arranged for Dad had already been filled. Floss still had the job for Mom. As usual, in explaining the bad news she took it very calmly but Dad was more than a bit put out.

Christmas 1966 saw only Mom in work. Dad, Sheila and me were all still looking for some form of employment. I gave the folks the only present I had to give - the £250 that lorry driver had given me. It was sort of mine - he never said anything about paying it back, said nothing but hold on to it.

I had no alternative but to help my folks out in times of need. They were over the Moon but asked where I'd got the money.

I told them the tale about the warehouse, also how I'd come by the money. Mom was worried that this money was only to be held by me and not spent.

I reminded her that we were now living in Weymouth and I'd never mentioned to anyone at the warehouse that we were moving here. This made my mom feel a bit easier. She thought it out and said that if we got jobs in the new year our first task would be to get the money back up to £250, so whatever was spent over Christmas, we would make up the balance.

The money was mostly spent but eventually got made back up. My dad finally got a job -at the local crematorium. Sheila went to work in an old folks' home, Mom left the job that Floss had got her and became a supervisor in a family-owned restaurant business. As for me, I worked for a local MP. He was good to me, helped me on my feet when things were down - even gave money to get myself some smart clobber. I never looked back. We stuck to our jobs for a good few years and eventually recovered something like the standard of living we had achieved in Birmingham.

Just after the 1969 holiday season, I left Weymouth for Germany but that's another story.

Above: Being hauled by a King between Snow Hill and Paddington was all part of the joy that went with a trip to London. No. 6008 *King James 11* gathers speed and leaves Paddington behind while returning an express to Birmingham and Wolverhampton. *(Photo by Robert Anderson)*

Below: The second photo I took with my new Brownie 127 camera during its first outing on 11th June, 1962. A pair of 'Consuls,' 48353 and 48218, stand behind the coal hopper at Saltley depot on 11th June, 1962.

We began so many of our great trips out by watching for the smoke of our train approaching Snow Hill from the Wolverhampton direction. This was that view just a bit before my spotting days in 1957 when Grange class 4-6-0 No. 6861 *Crynant Grange* was approaching with a goods train. *(Photo by T. J. Edgington / Colourail)*

Above: Bushbury shed, 21C, with a good selection of engines on 22nd April, 1962, including a Black Five 4-6-0 and a Class 2 mogul. *(R.S.Carpenter photos)*

Below: Class 9F 2-10-0 No. 92232 looks nice and clean as it emerges from Oxley shed, Wolverhampton, on a bright day in 1962. *(B. Metcalfe / Colourail)*

Above: Bitannia Pacific No. 70052 *Firth of Tay* takes centre stage at Crewe South shed on 5th September, 1965. Jinty 0-6-0Ts are on the right and another Britannia, and Jubilee No. 45565 *Victoria* in with a railtour from Bradford, are on the left. *(Jack Wild / Stephen Chapman collection)*

Below: Most Western engines visiting Crewe congregated at the little Gresty Lane sub-shed, seen here on 30th March, 1958 with Prairie tank No. 4120 and what looks like a County 4-6-0 tucked inside. *(Photo by Graham Kaye)*

Above: No matter how you looked at it, there was just nothing to compare with the big red Coronation Pacifics at Crewe North shed. No. 46248 *City of Leeds* stands over the ash pit on 2nd December, 1962. *(Photo by Graham Kaye)*

Below: A packed shed yard like this one, 36E Retford, was a wonderful sight for any spotter - 14 engines on view just in this bit of the depot and a good variety too. *(N.E.Stead collection)*

Above: The one occasion we accepted a lift with a stranger we were lucky that this was where it got us - Kirkby-in-Ashfield shed with "Consuls" 48063 and 48124 flanking a diesel shunter on 24th April, 1966. *(Photo by Adrian Booth)*

Below: Annesley shed on 30th August, 1964. Eamon Crawley(left), Gerry Williams and (right) Nicky "The Bounce" Hand with rebuilt Patriot 4-6-0 No. 45535 *Sir Herbert Walker KCB. (Photo by Alex Scott)*

Above: The brooding atmosphere of a big roundhouse often brought on an attack of butterflies in the pit of my stomach as we wandered gingerly round the locos. This was Leeds Holbeck with a pair of Ivatt Class 4 moguls, a 9F 2-10-0, a Fowler 2-6-4T and a Drewry diesel shunter grouped round the turntable.
(Photo by Arthur Chester)

Below: Oxford shed was bunked a good few times. Hall class 4-6-0 No. 6976 *Graythwaite Hall* was near the coal stage on 18th November, 1957.
(Photo by Graham Kaye)

Above: The Somerset and Dorset line was always something a bit special with some interesting locos but it took a coach trip for me to reach out-of-the-way Templecombe shed. On this particular day in 1963, the yard was occupied by S&D 7F 2-8-0 No. 53806, a 4F 0-6-0, BR Class 5 4-6-0 No. 73050 and a Great Western Collett 2251 class 0-6-0. *(Jack Wild / Stephen Chapman collection)*

Below: Where it all ended. The date is 10th July, 1967, the yard at Weymouth shed is full of dumped engines, and the age of steam on the Southern Region has come to an end. *(Photo by Peter Shipman)*